LADIES FIRST

A PHOTOGRAPHIC ESSAY ON

GENDER EXPECTATIONS

IAN HOSKIN

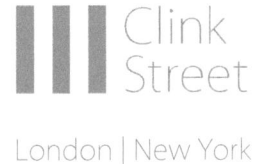

London | New York

Published by Clink Street Publishing 2017

Copyright © 2017

First edition.

The authors assert the moral right under the Copyright, Designs and Patents Act 1988 to be identified as the authors of this work.

All rights reserved. No part of this publication may be reproduced, stored in a retrieval system or transmitted, in any form or by any means without the prior consent of the author, nor be otherwise circulated in any form of binding or cover other than that with which it is published and without a similar condition being imposed on the subsequent purchaser.

ISBN: 978-1-912262-51-9
E-Book: 978-1-912262-52-6

Dedication

Gina, without you there would be nothing to see.

xi

LADIES FIRST

Ladies First looks at the way society stereotypically views and places differing expectations on women and men. The title of the series of images plays on a traditional phrase most often used to indicate the custom of women being served first and allowed to exit or enter first, a privilege granted by men.

None of the views expressed in the text below the images are my own. They have all been identified from conversation, social interaction, the workplace, politics, advertising, radio, Television, literature and magazines. Viewed in conjunction with the images, the texts, wherever possible, are the same to highlight the differing ways we perceive and treat women and men. Informing these images is the important and topical issue of what are the defining factors that make up femininity and masculinity.

Some assumptions about gender are based on societal norms and peer groups, while others on an outdated view of evolutionary biology. Are women really programmed by their biology to care for children and the elderly while their man metaphorically chase dinner across the Savannah? There is a vestige of this thinking still current in our society and that thinking is just as relevant between the two genders as it is within each one: Much of the social pressure to conform to gender stereotypes comes from within a same-sex group.

The series of images was started in 1980 and after a gap of 35 years I did have to ask myself if it would still be relevant, but with the continuing lack of women in top jobs, issues like television's "Sofagate" and most recently the BBC's gender pay inequality, coupled with the nontraditional way I had chosen to live in the intervening years, I realised it had become more important to contribute to the dialogue on the issue of gender. As one area of gender inequality is pinned down with legislation another one takes its place.

The original series had no text and many of the original images have been discarded, words added and the series expanded to accommodate as many of the issues of gender difference I could identify and plausibly translate into images.

I was born in Newcastle in the North East of England. On moving to London in the early 1980's some people I met were surprised to discover that I was English as their exposure to regional accents was very limited. They were confused when I mentioned that I found them difficult to understand, because as Londoners they assumed they spoke with no accent. I want to do the equivalent with this work and question what we see as the norm by examining an inherited set of values that is accepted as natural and normal by society but is both prescriptive and limiting.

Ian Hoskin. 2017.

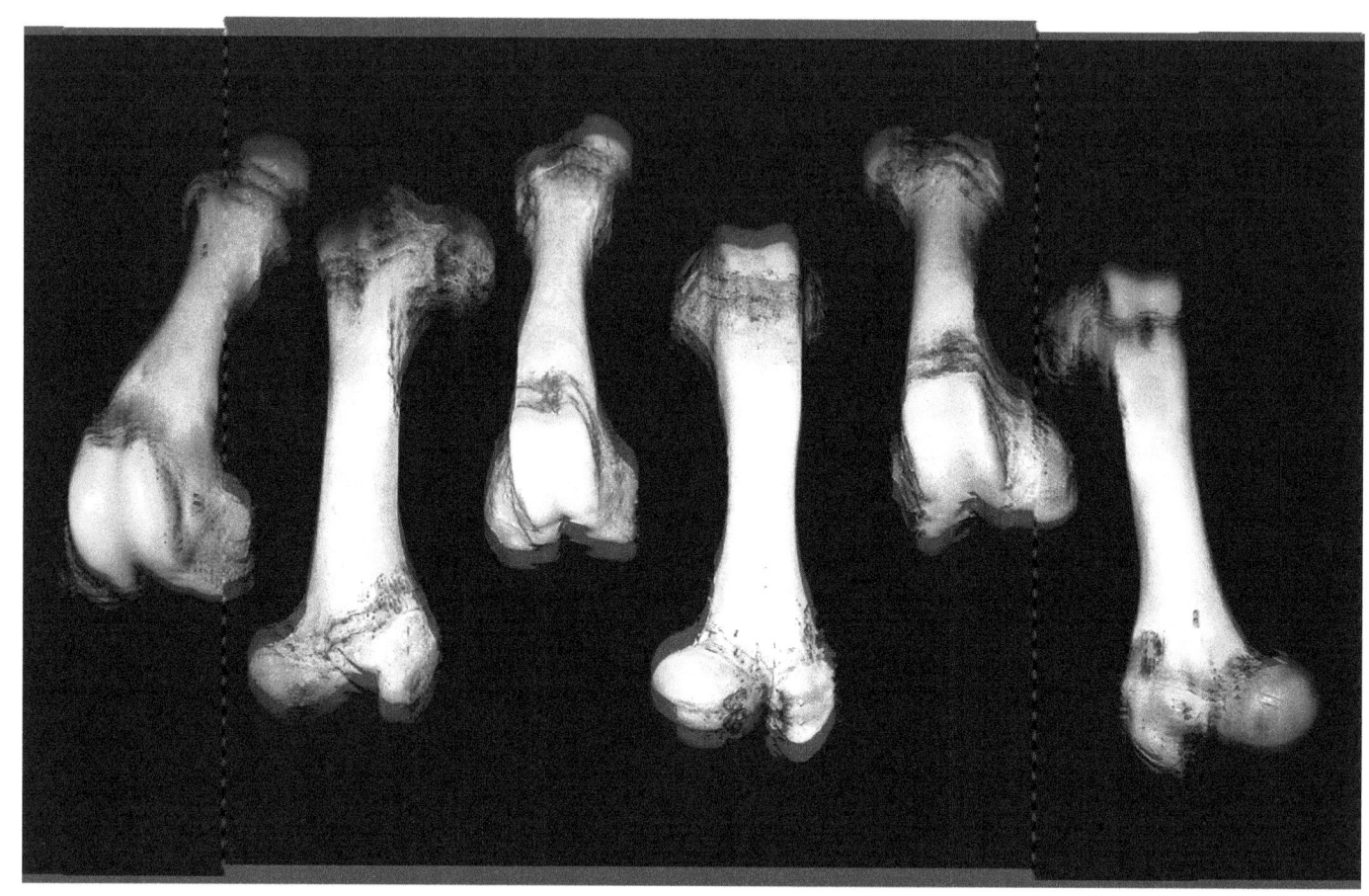

She intuitively understands how things work.
She intuitively understands how things work.

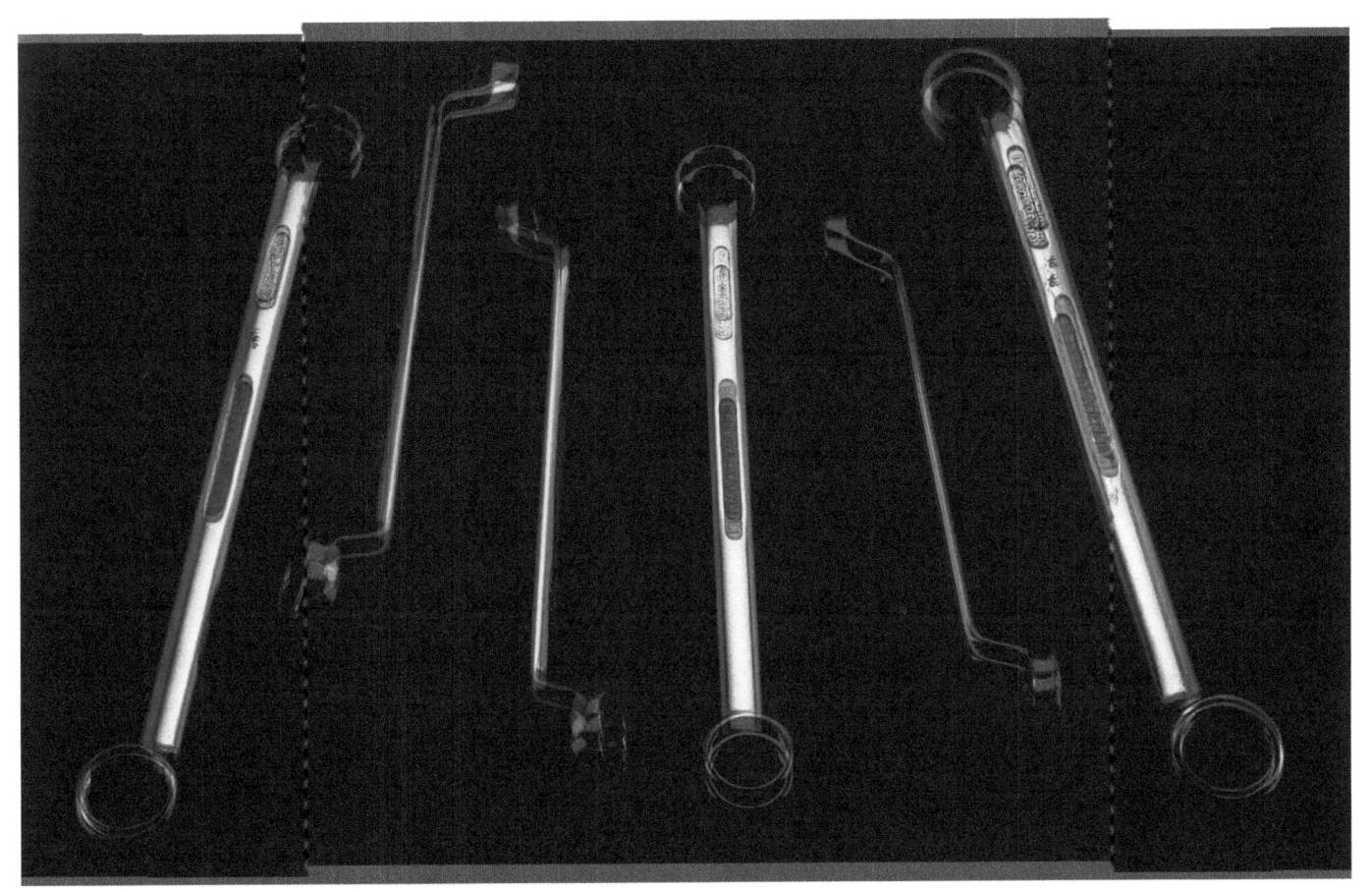

He intuitively understands how things work.
He intuitively understands how things work.

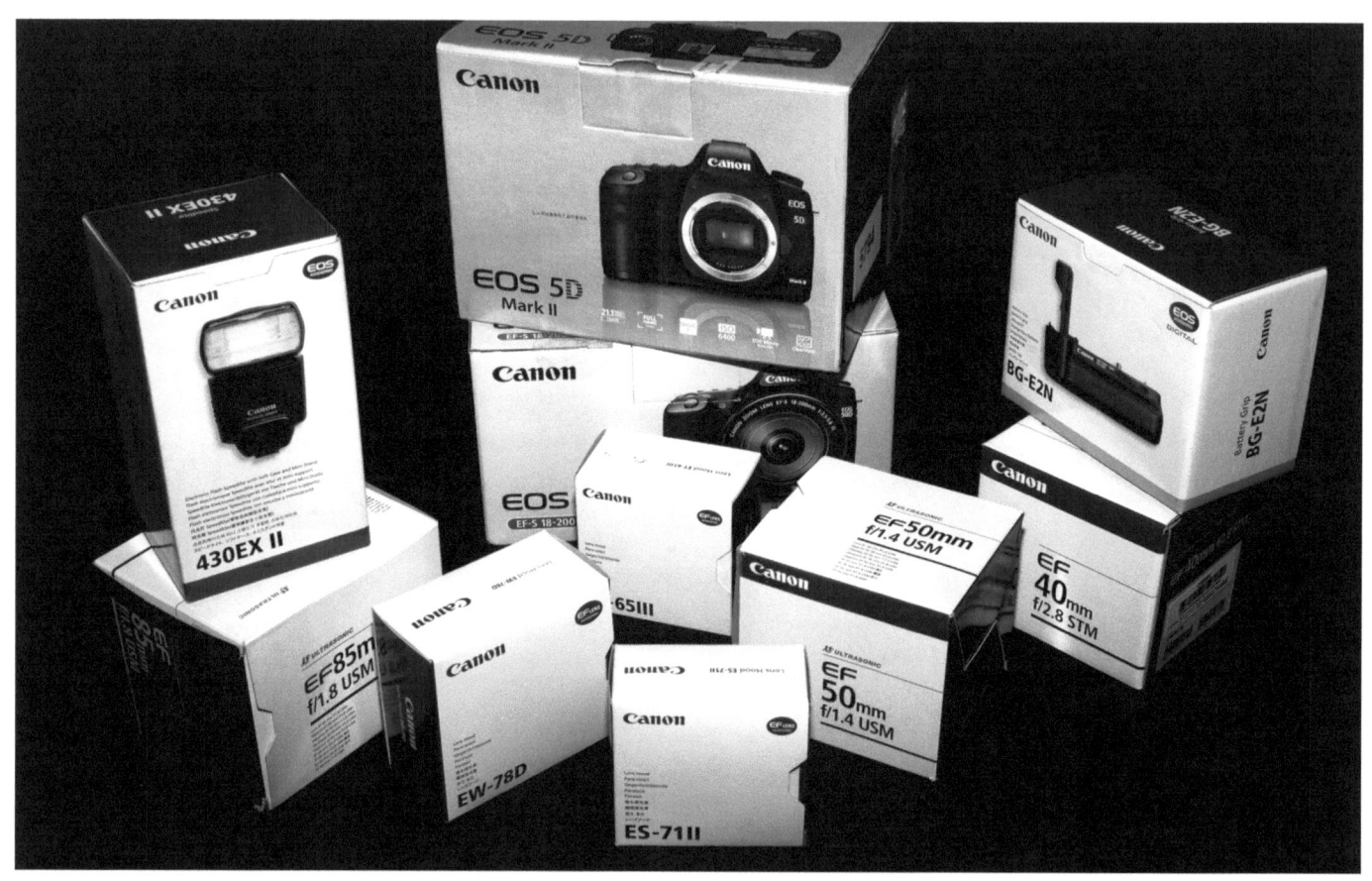

She thought he spent extravagantly.

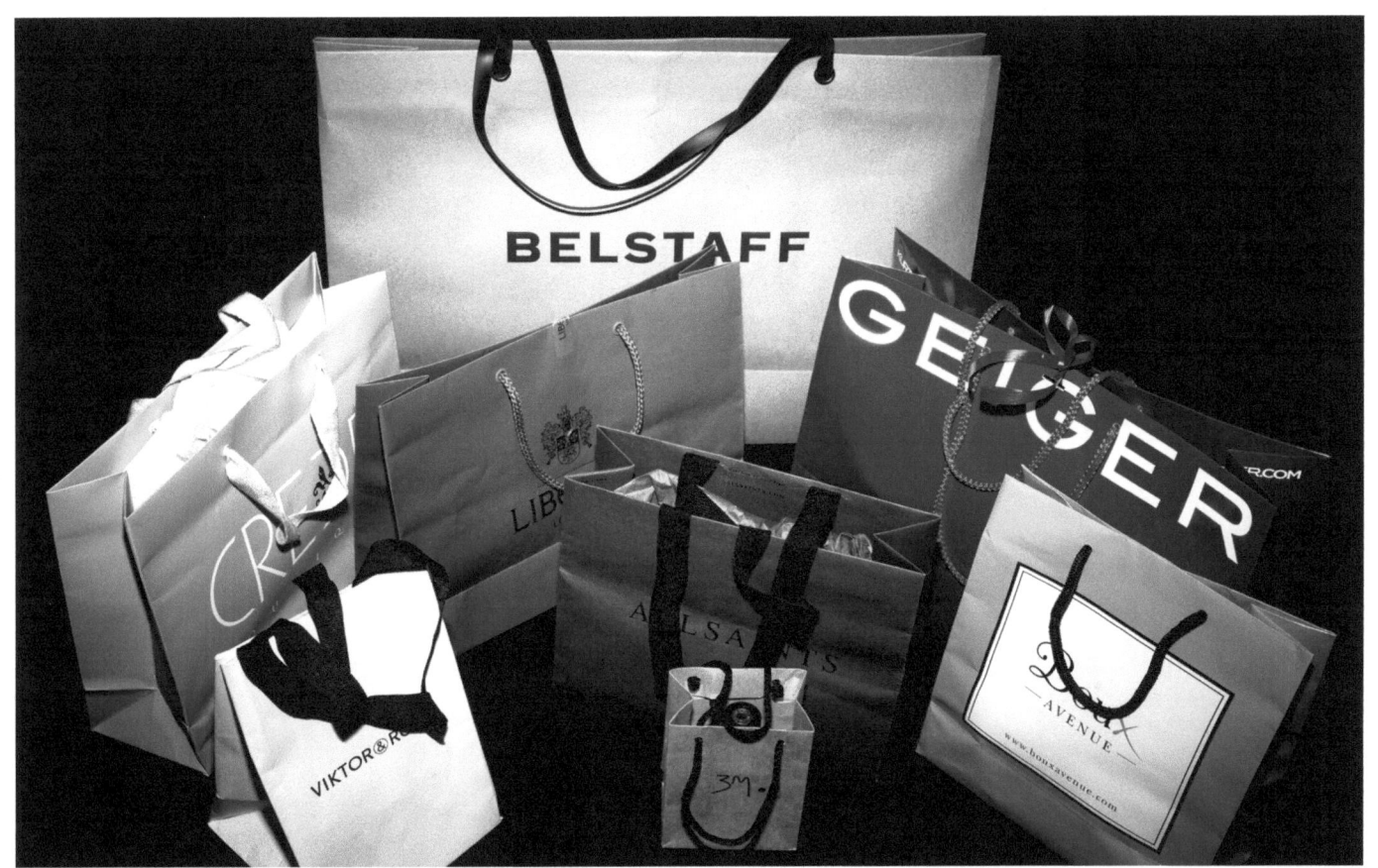

He thought she spent extravagantly.

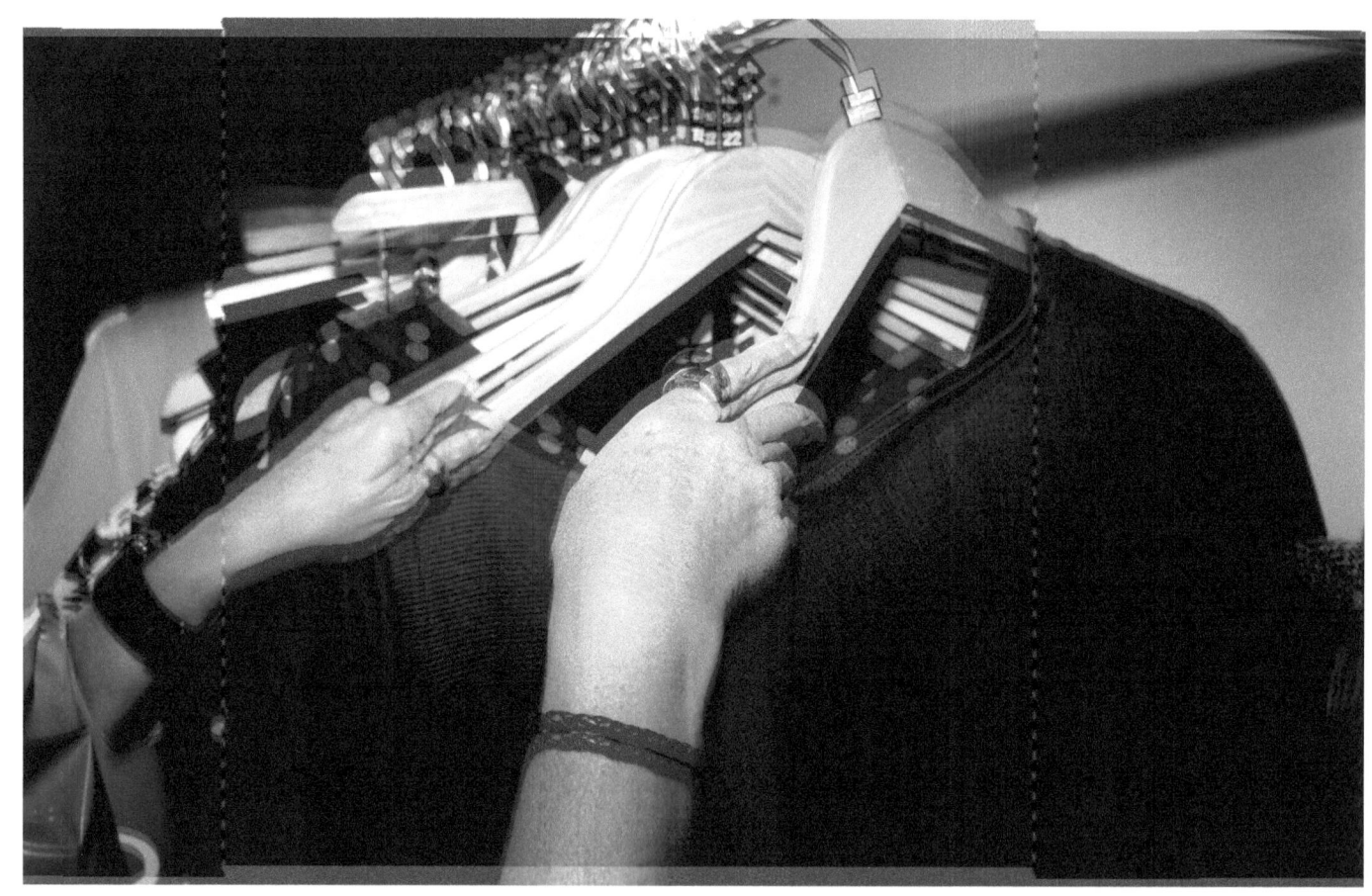

She enjoys hunting.
She enjoys hunting.

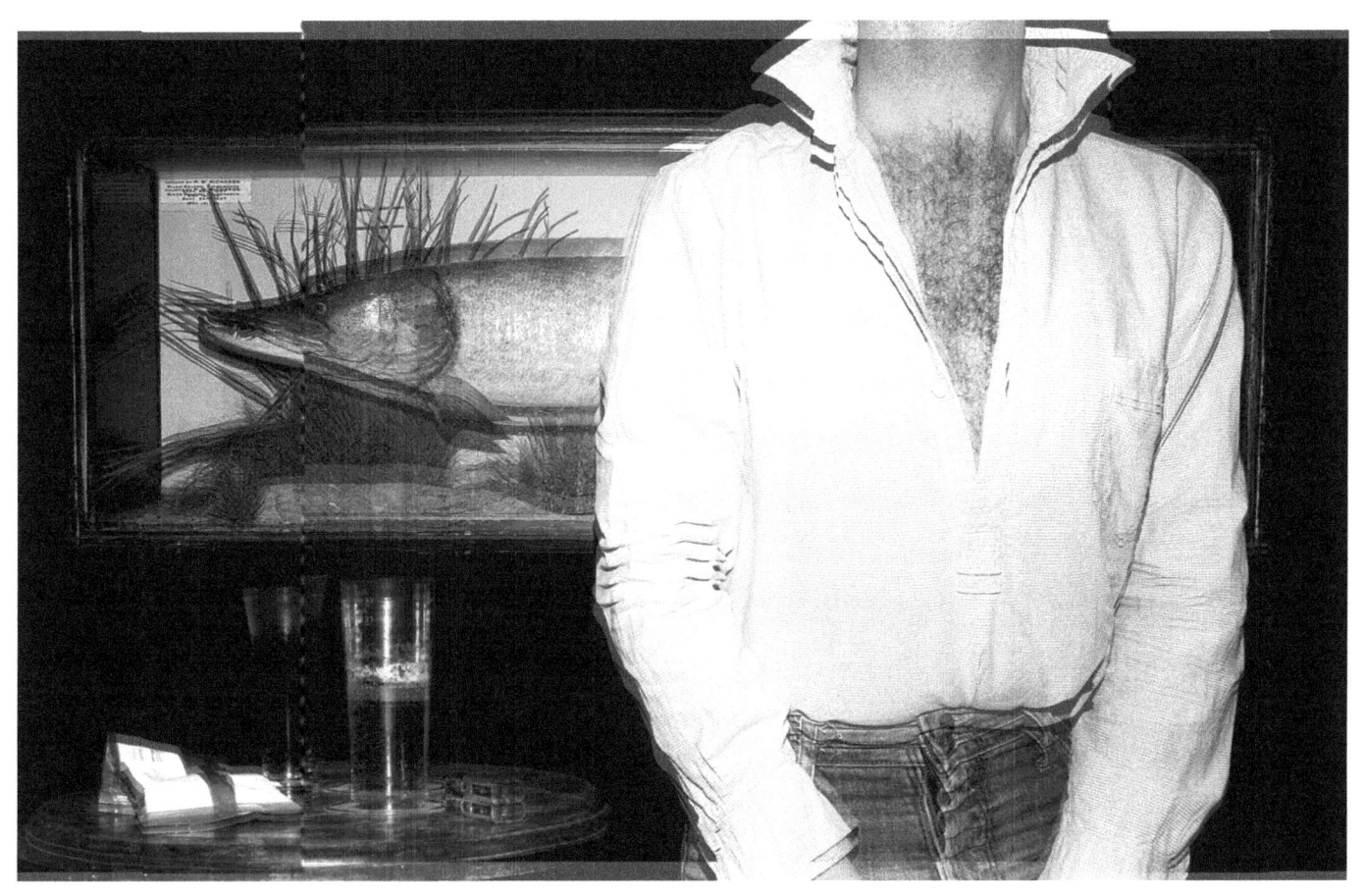

He enjoys hunting.
He enjoys hunting.

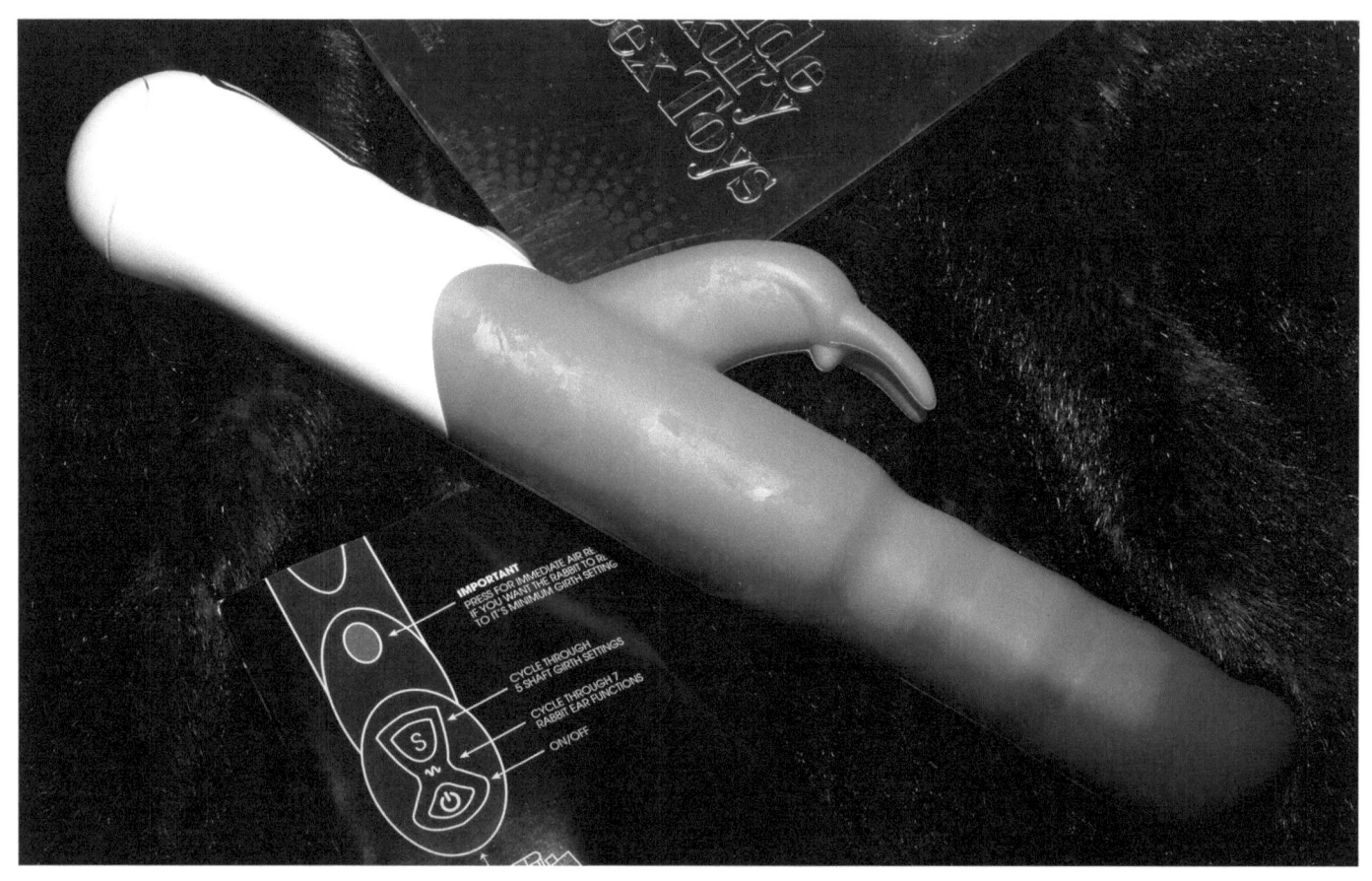

She sometimes still plays with toys.

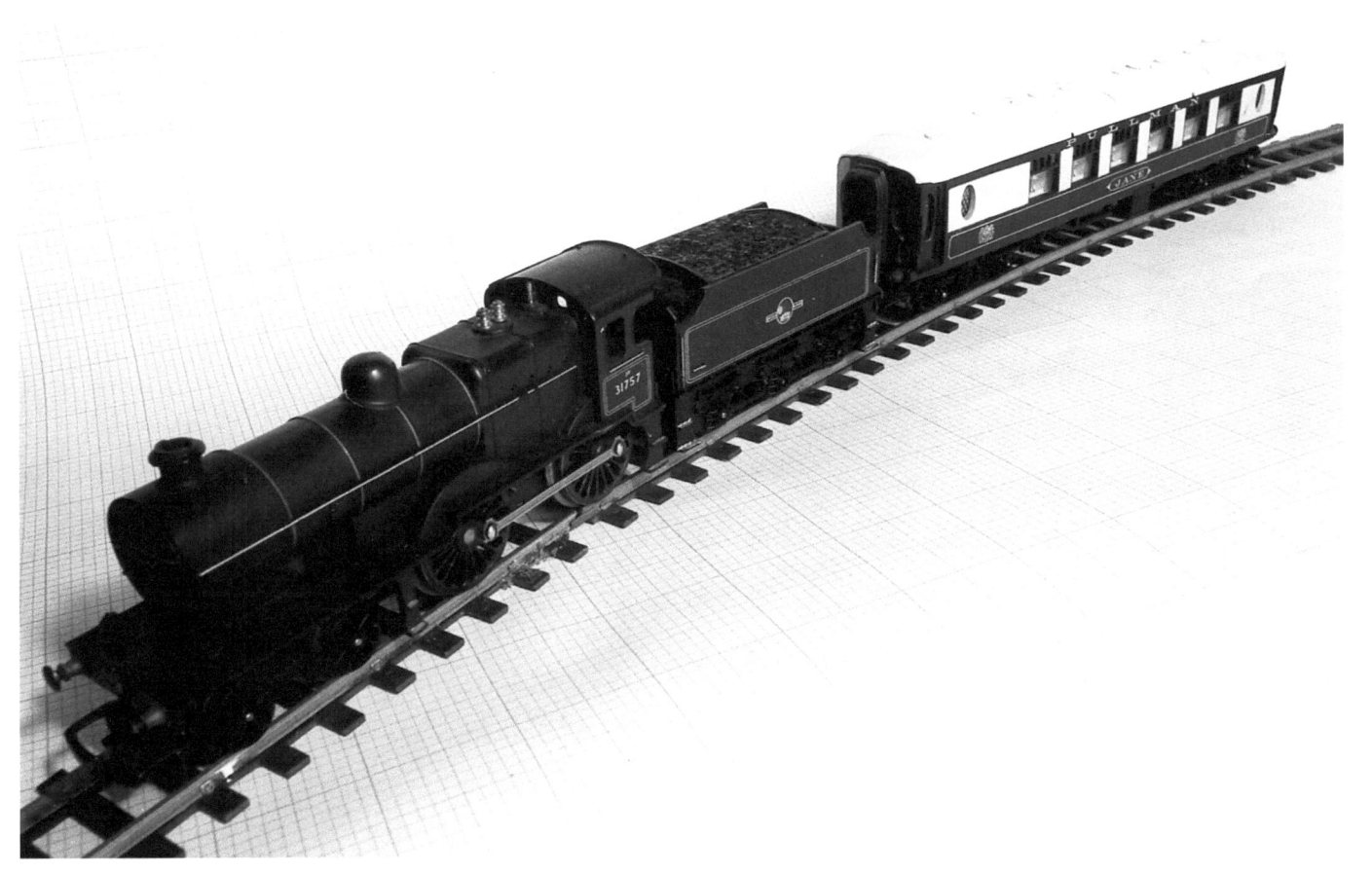

He sometimes still plays with toys.

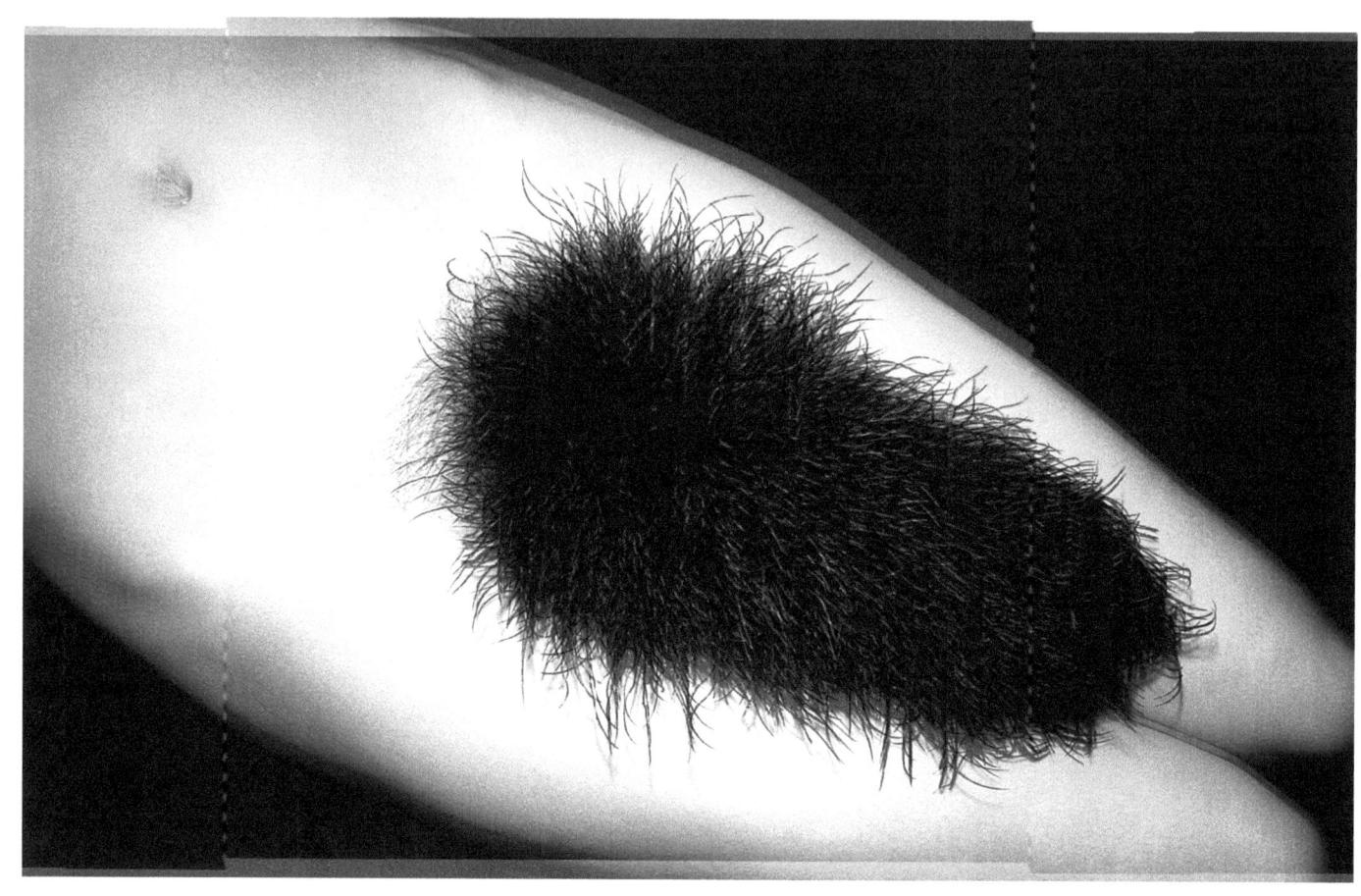

She has concerns about her hair.
She has concerns about her hair.

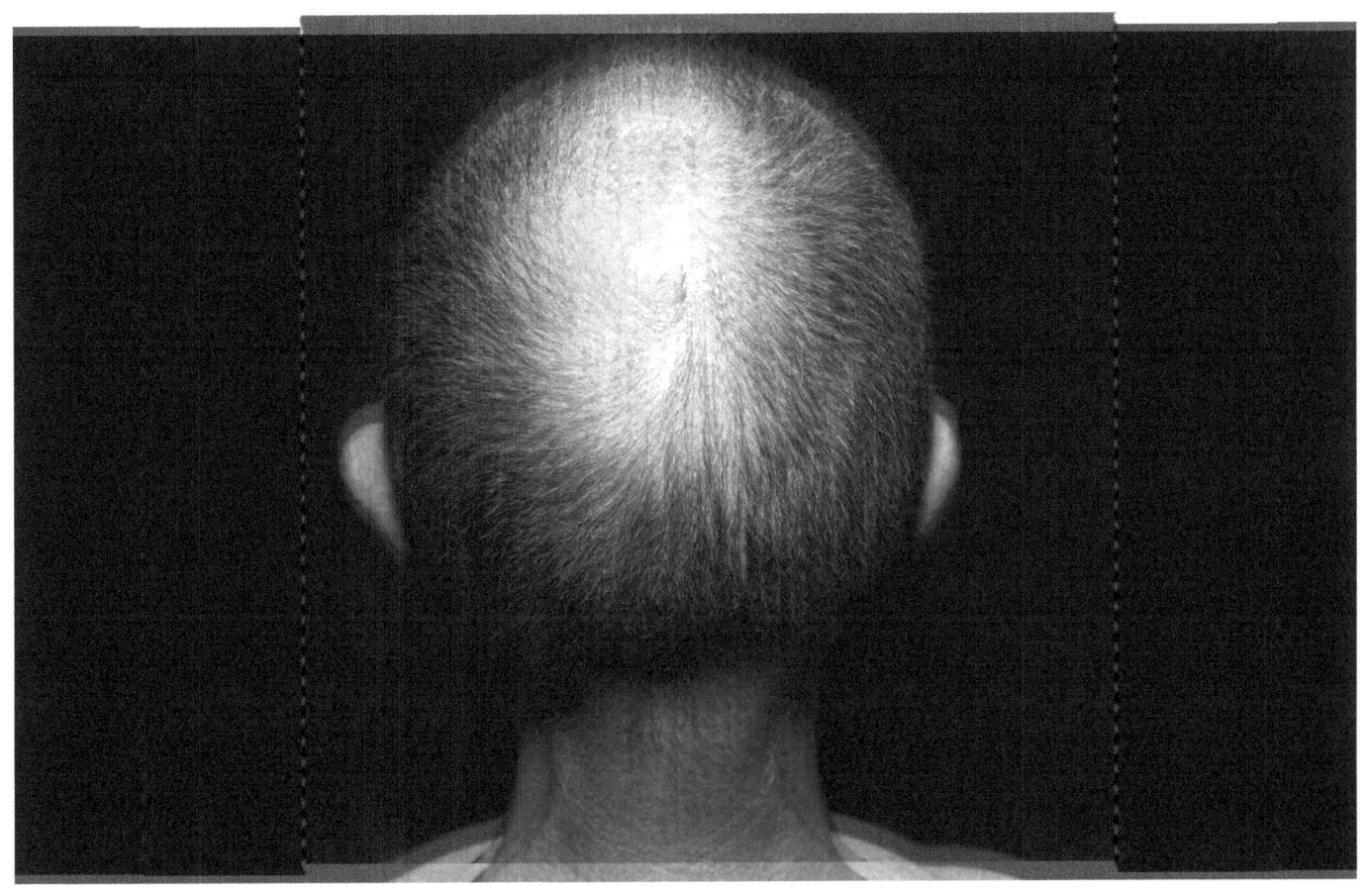

He has concerns about his hair.
He has concerns about his hair.

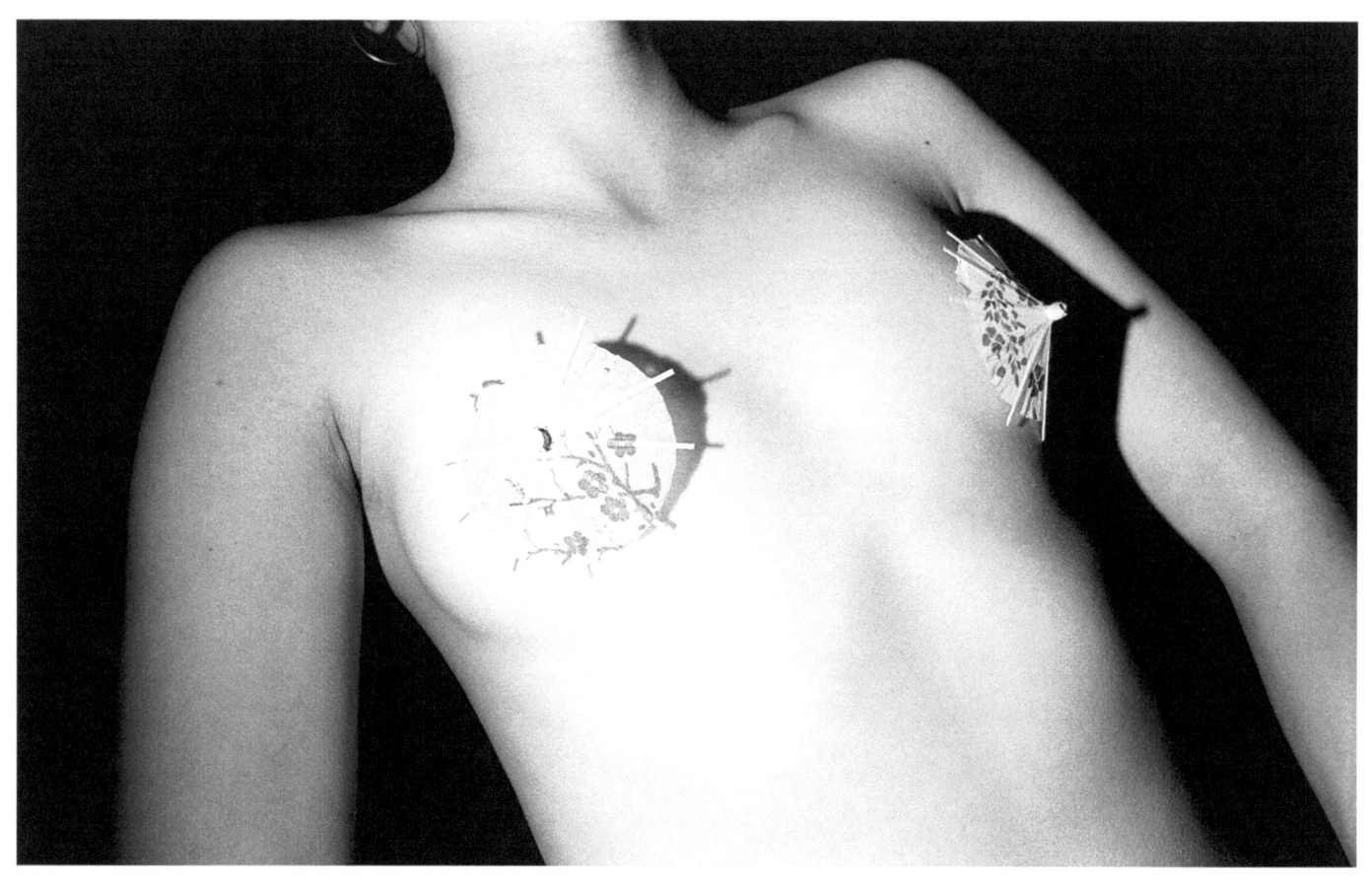

She is always in two minds about topless sunbathing.

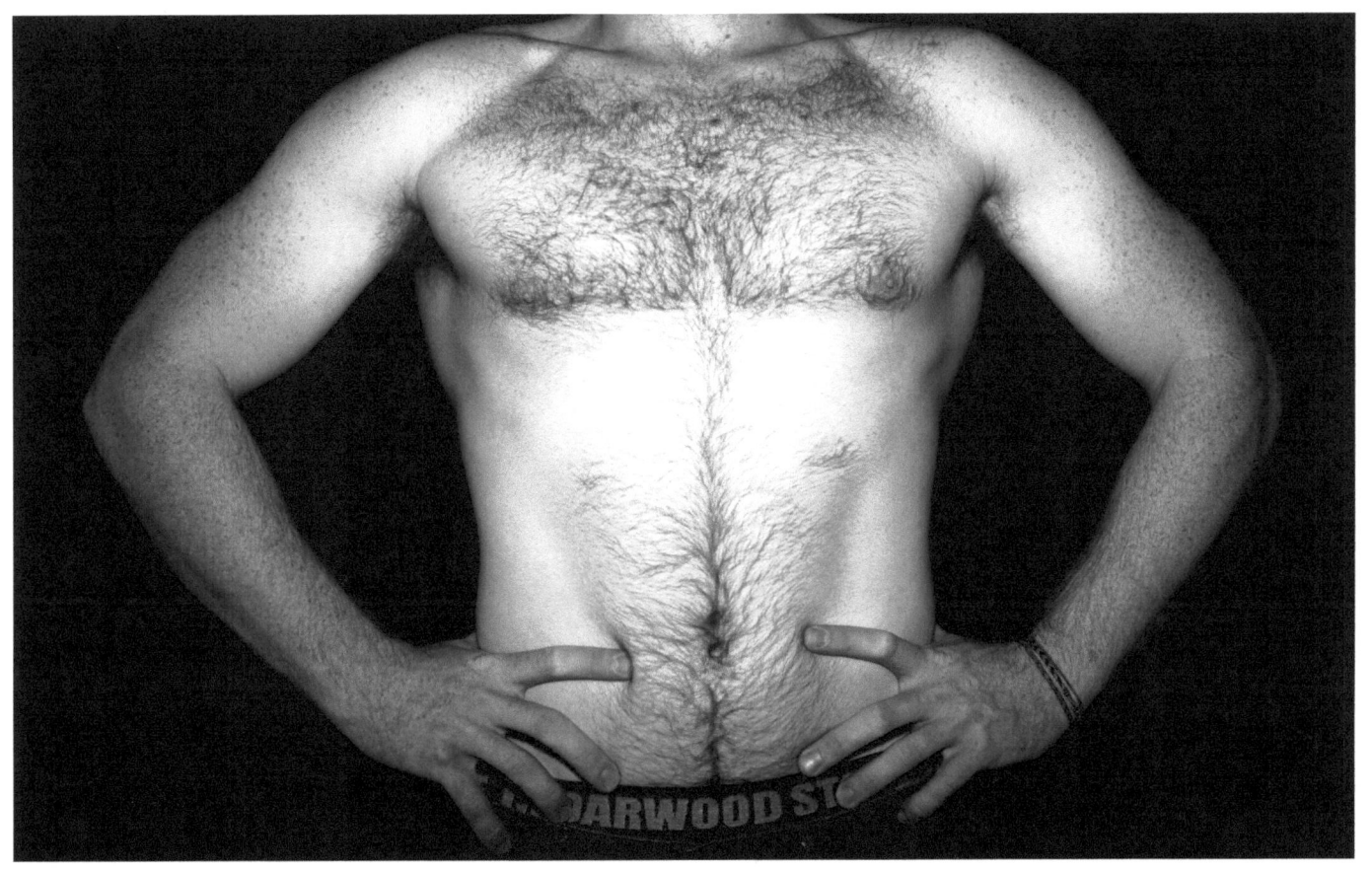

He is always in two minds about topless sunbathing.

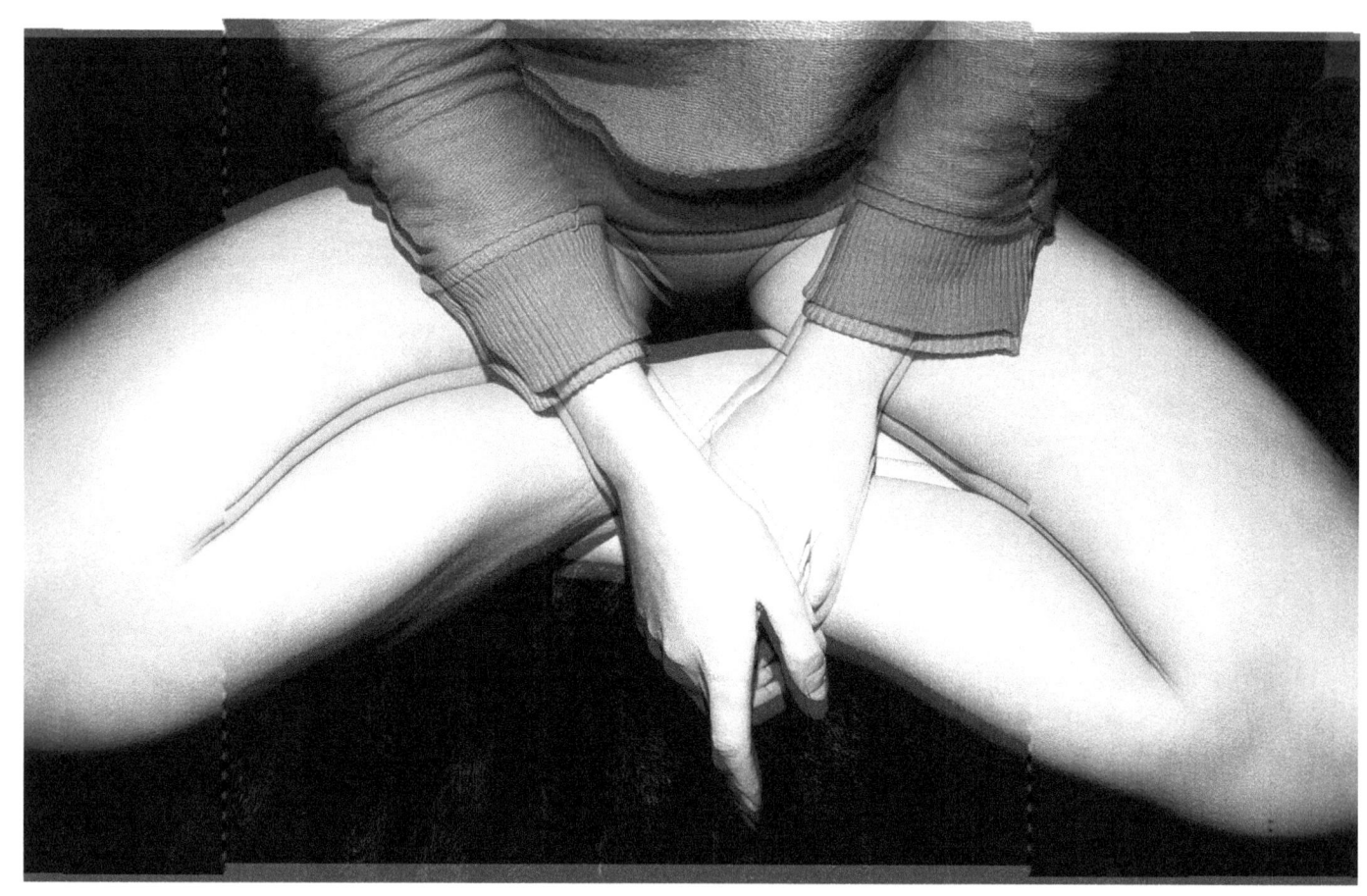

She feels 21 is a very good age.
She feels 21 is a very good age.

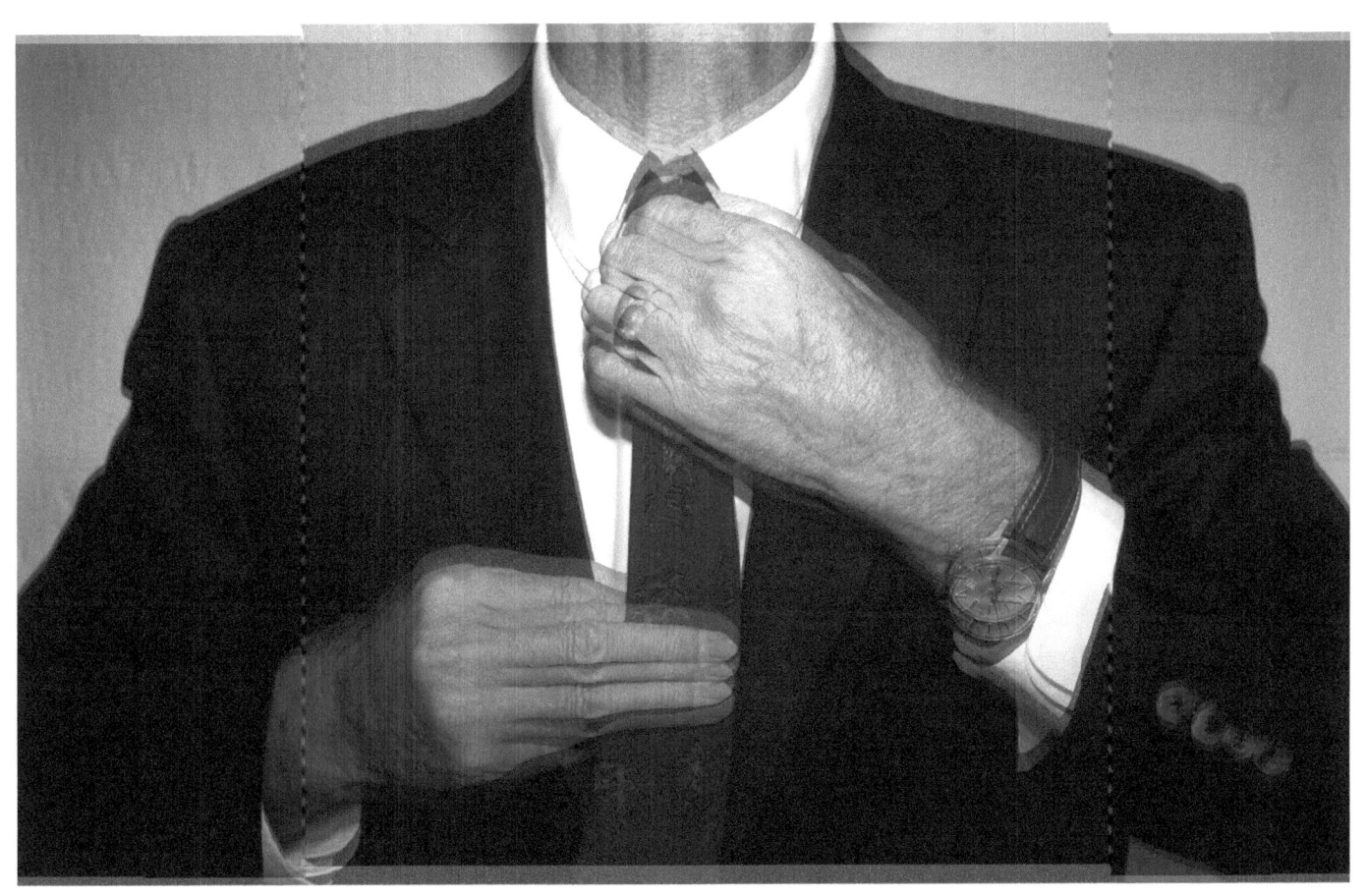

He feels 21 is a very good age.
He feels 21 is a very good age.

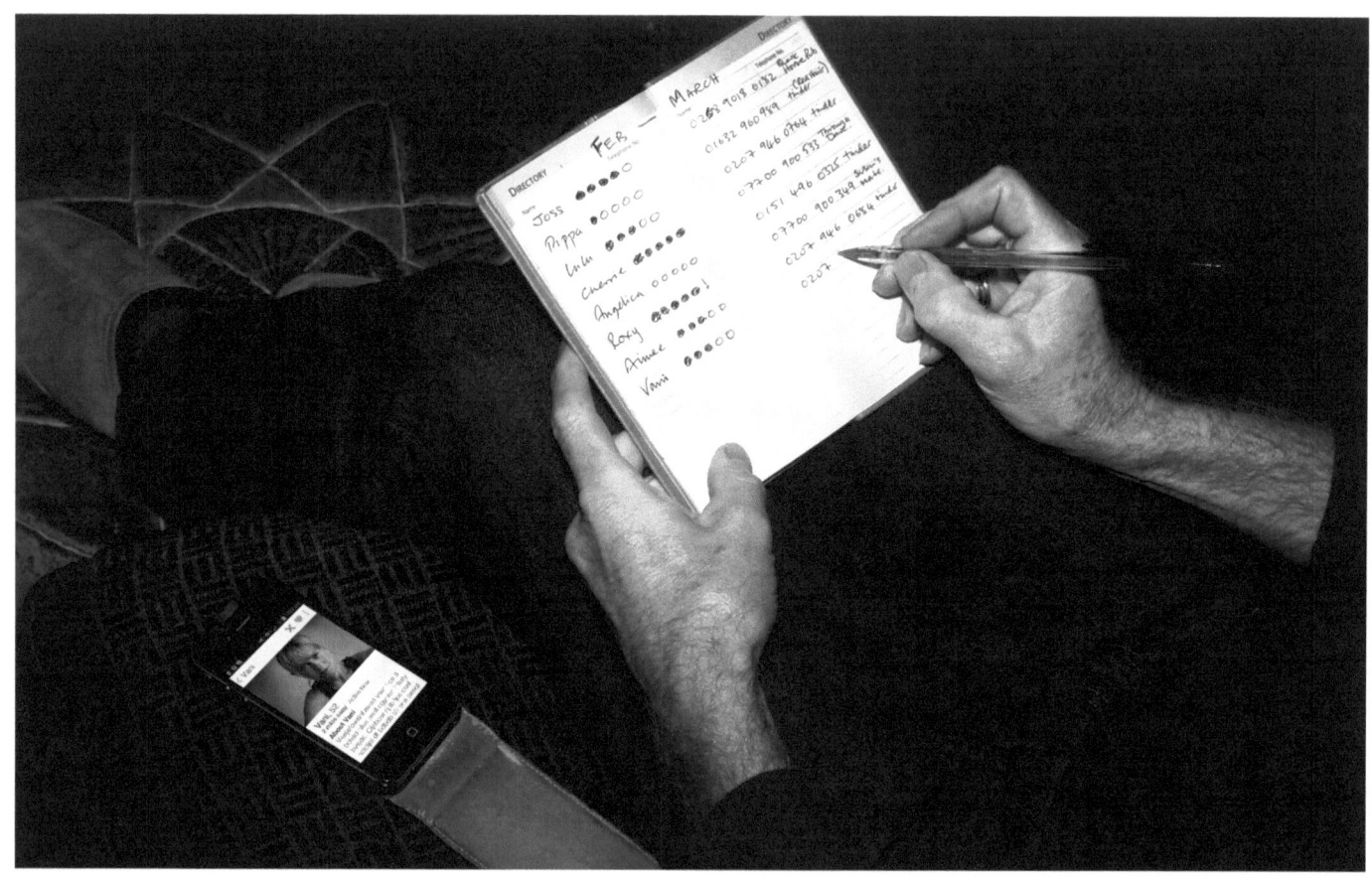

She believes that men wanting sex more than women is terribly common.

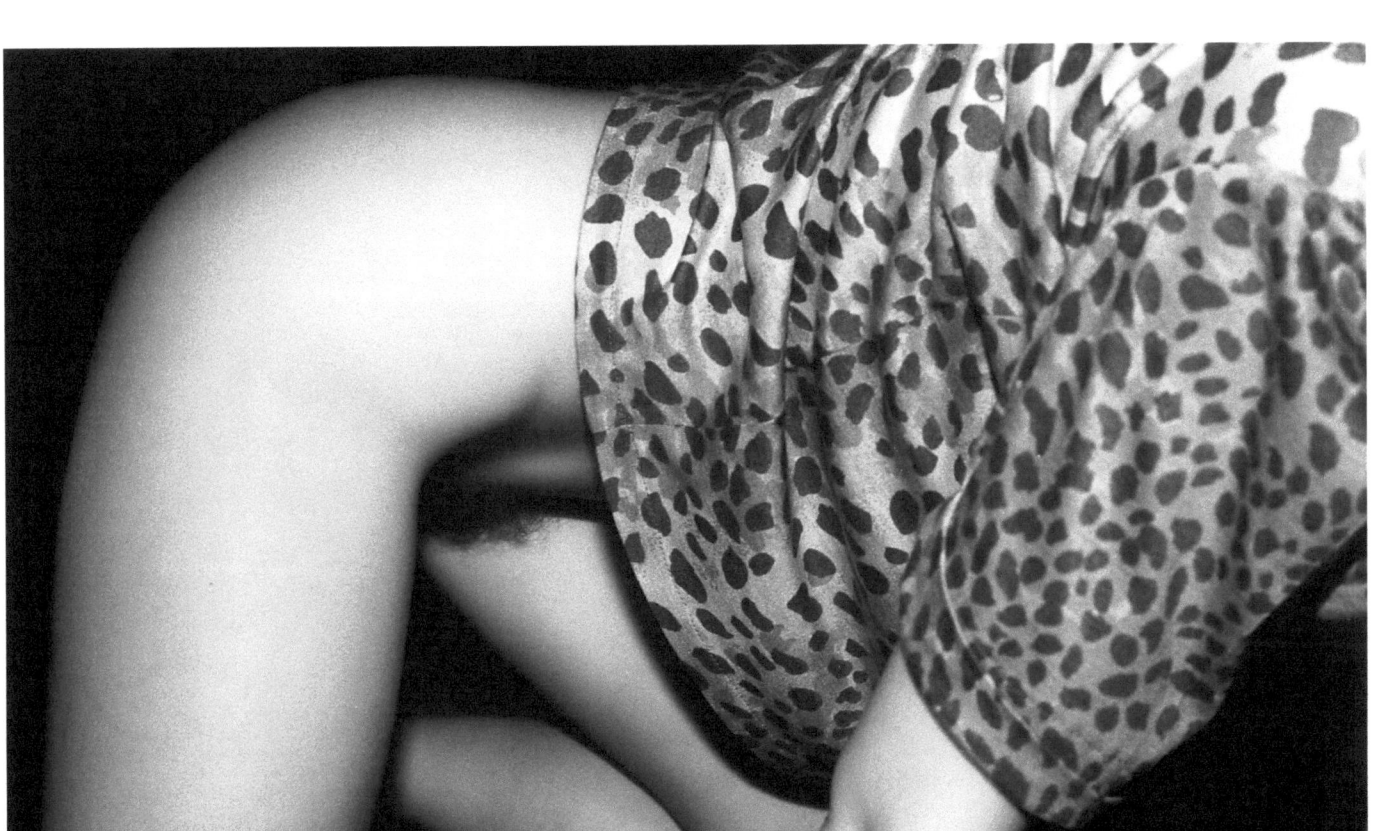

He believes that women wanting sex more than men is terribly common.

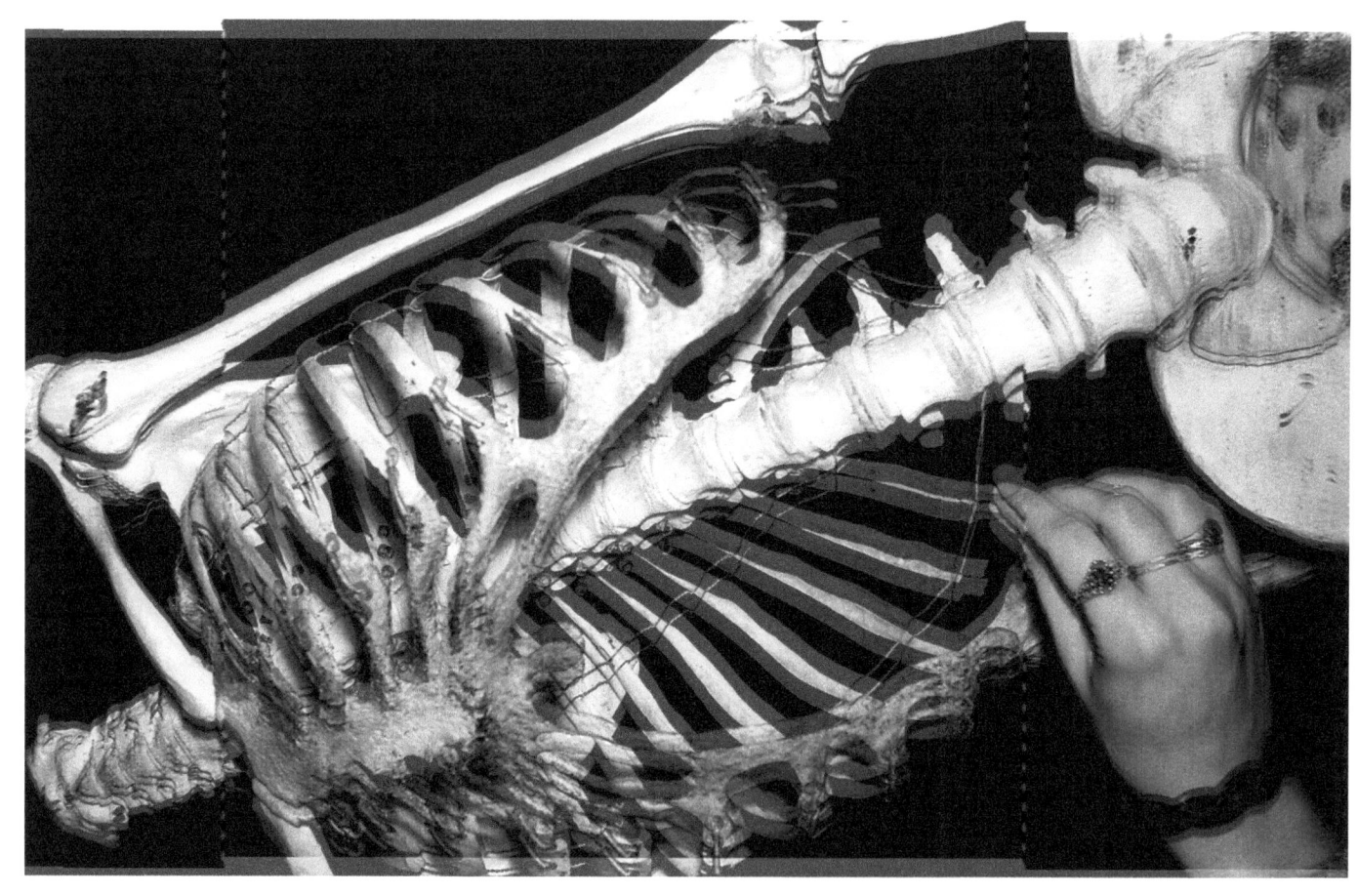

She studied anatomy carefully.
She studied anatomy carefully.

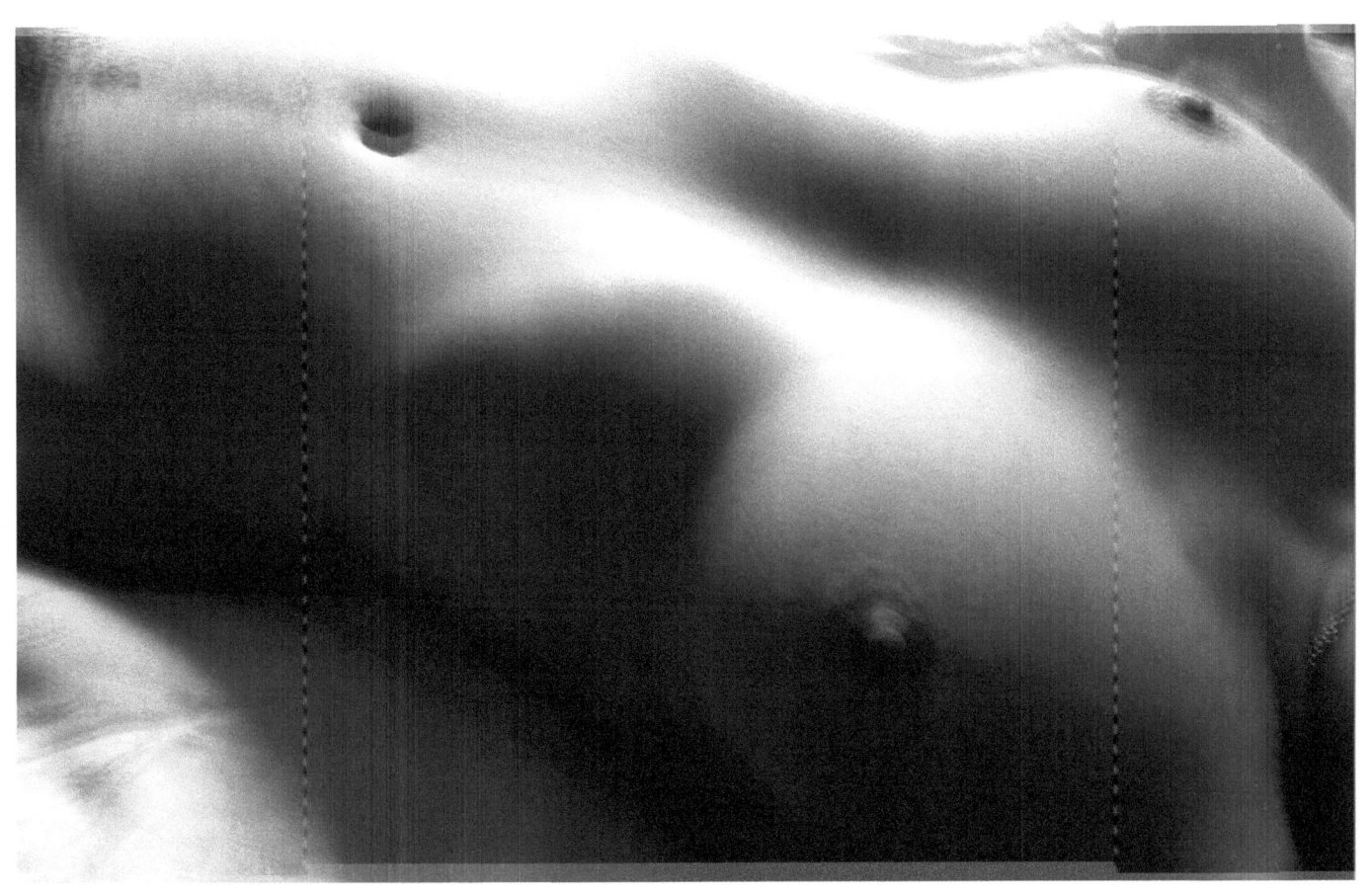

He studied anatomy carefully.

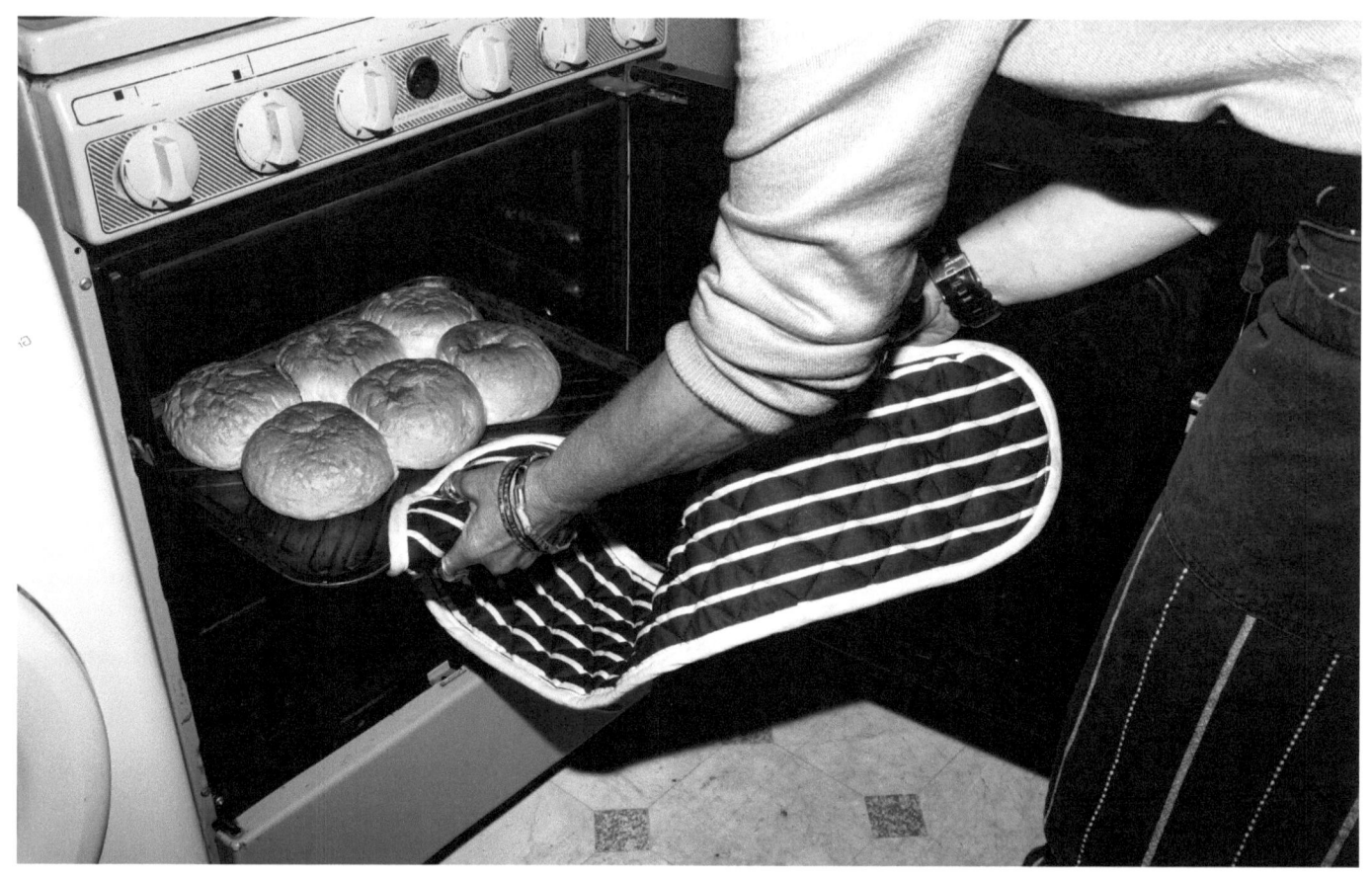

She opens doors for him.

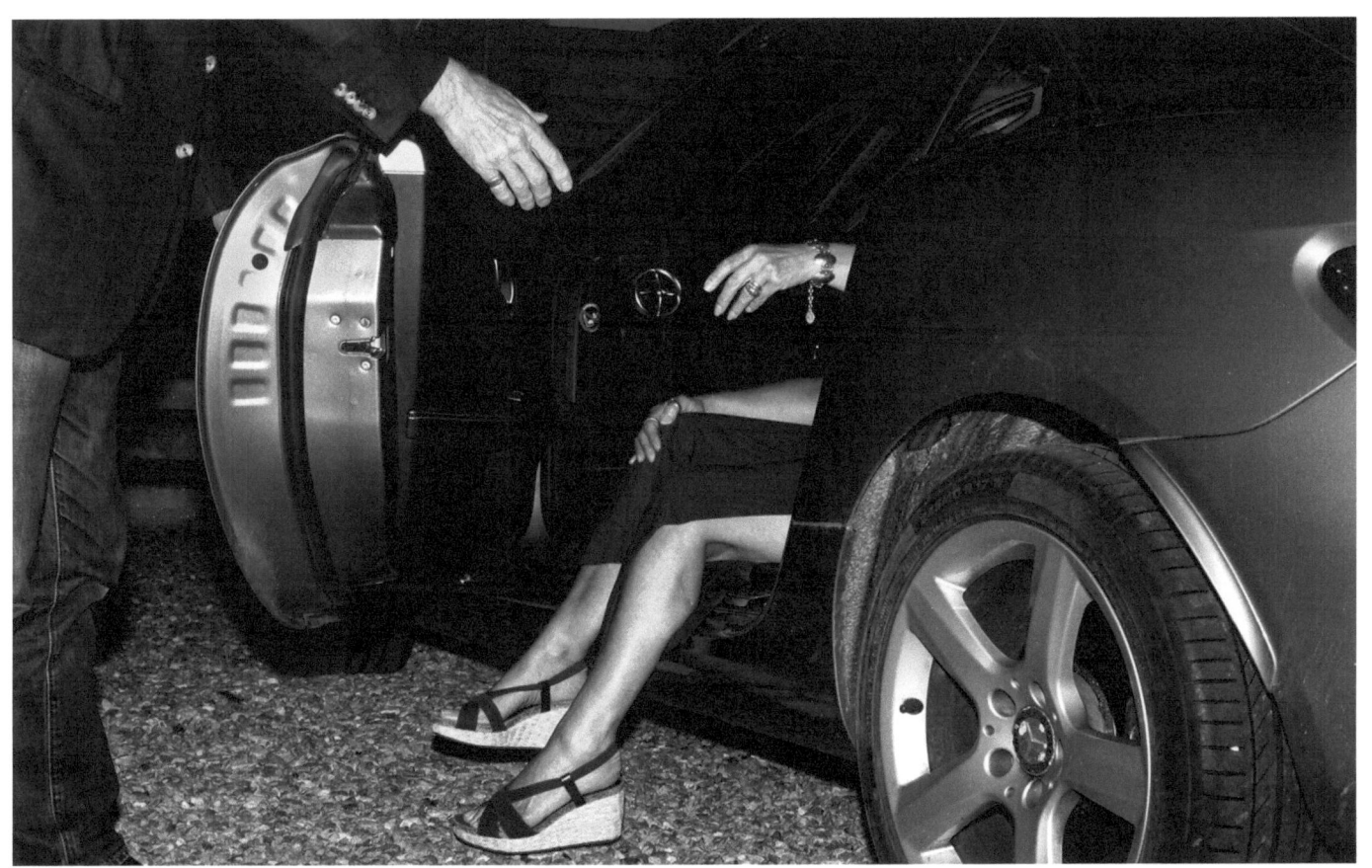

He opens doors for her.

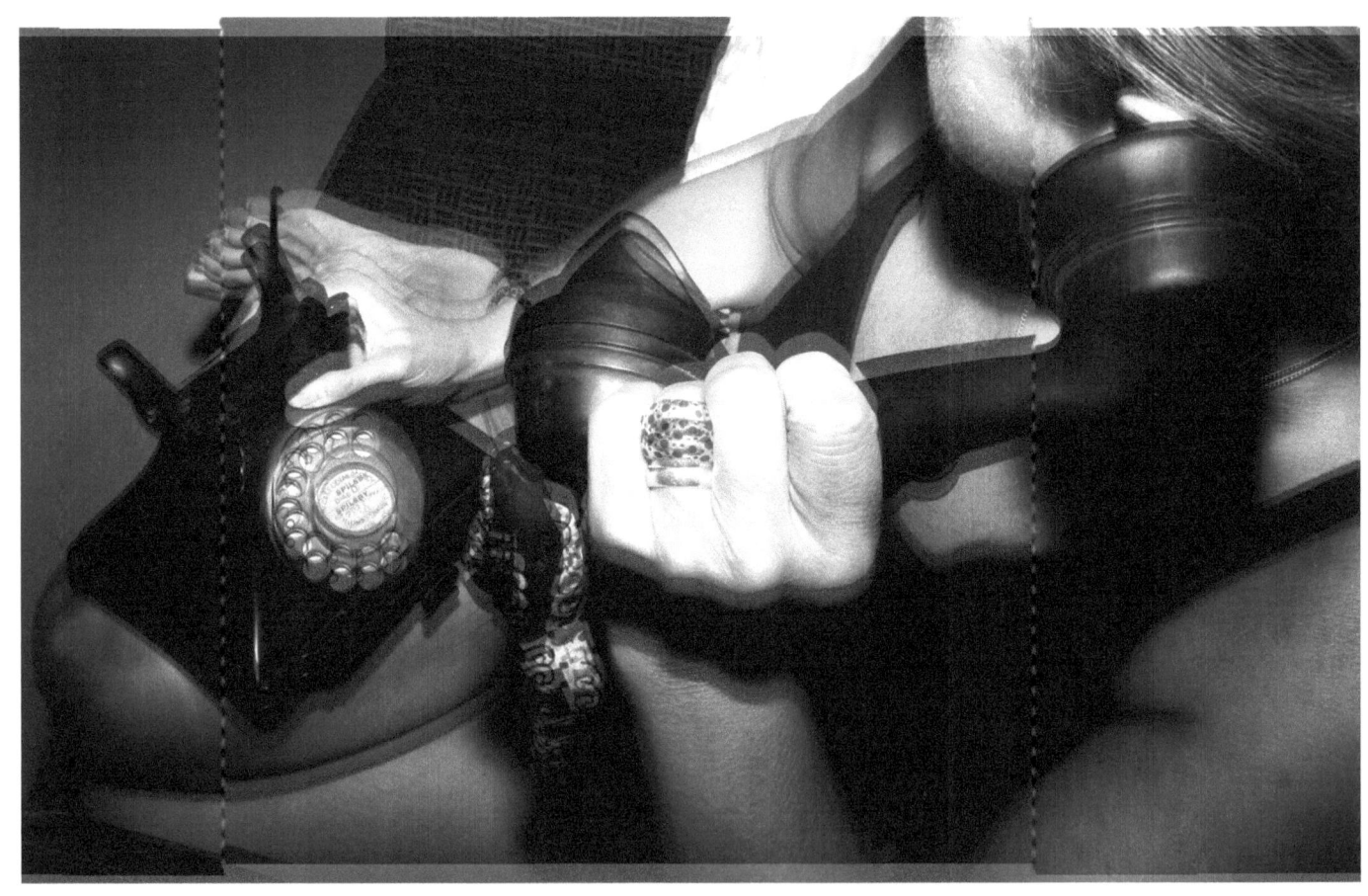

She takes satisfaction in finding solutions.
She takes satisfaction in finding solutions.

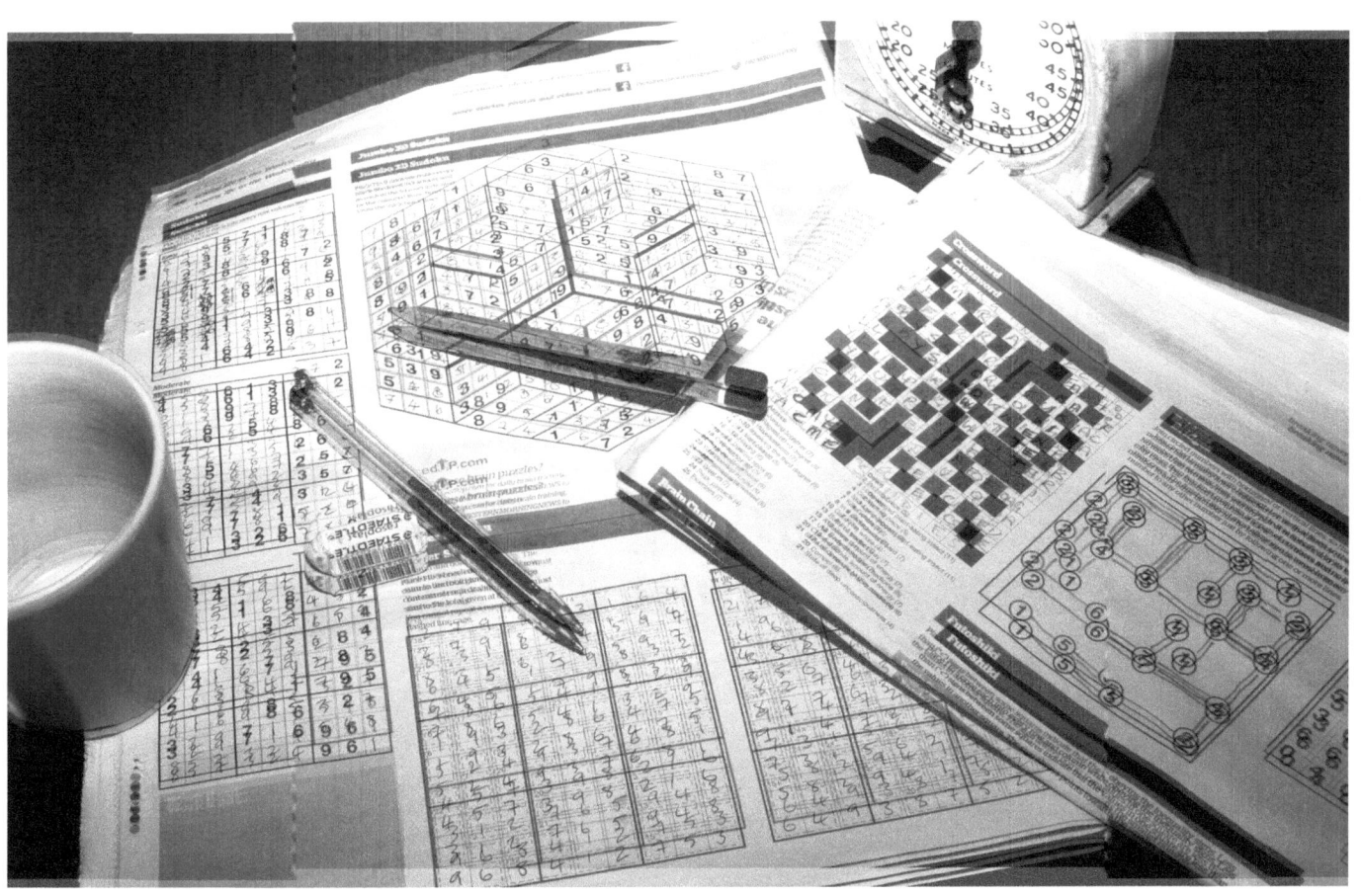

He takes satisfaction in finding solutions.

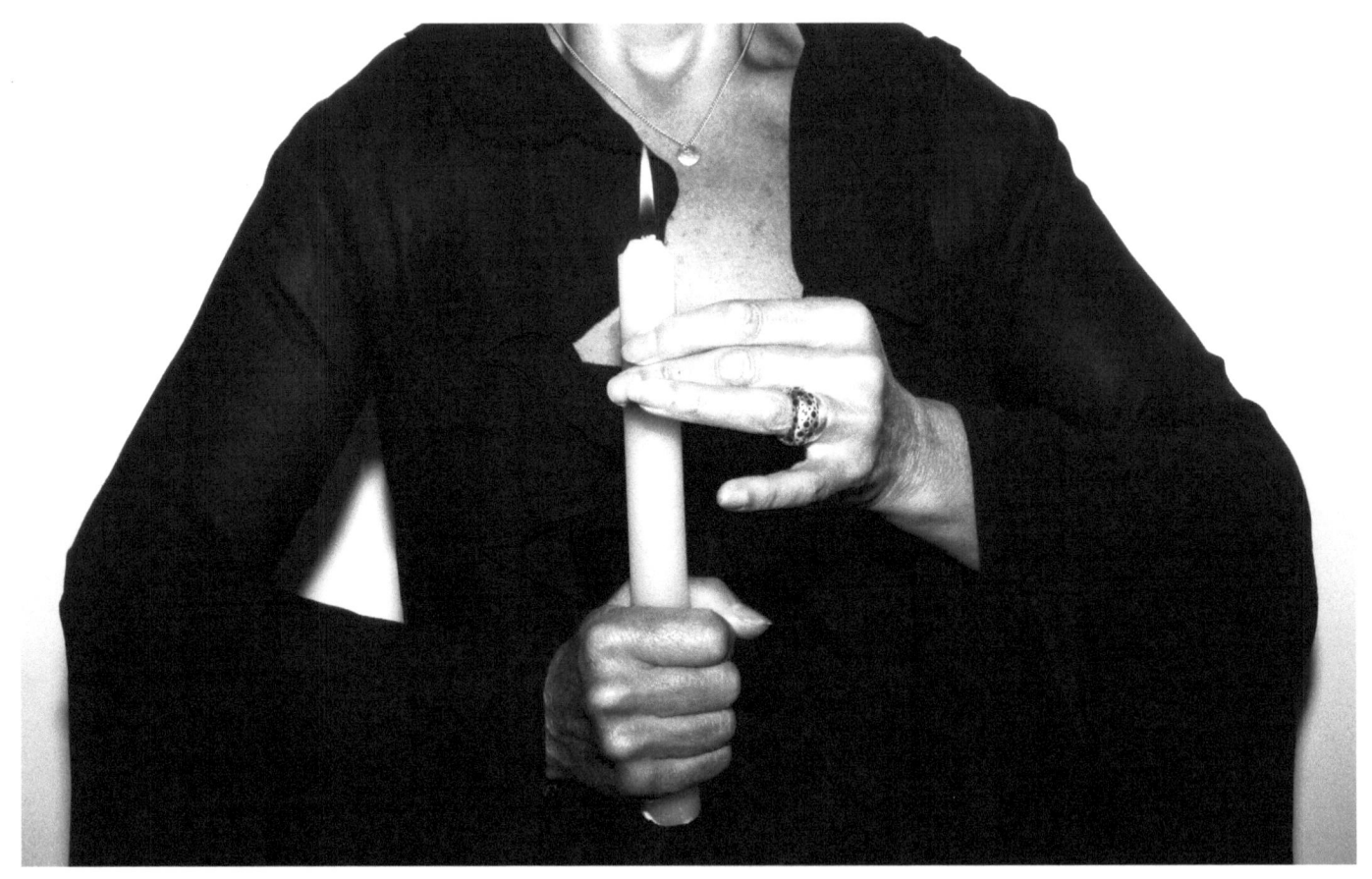

She prefers to light the bedroom.

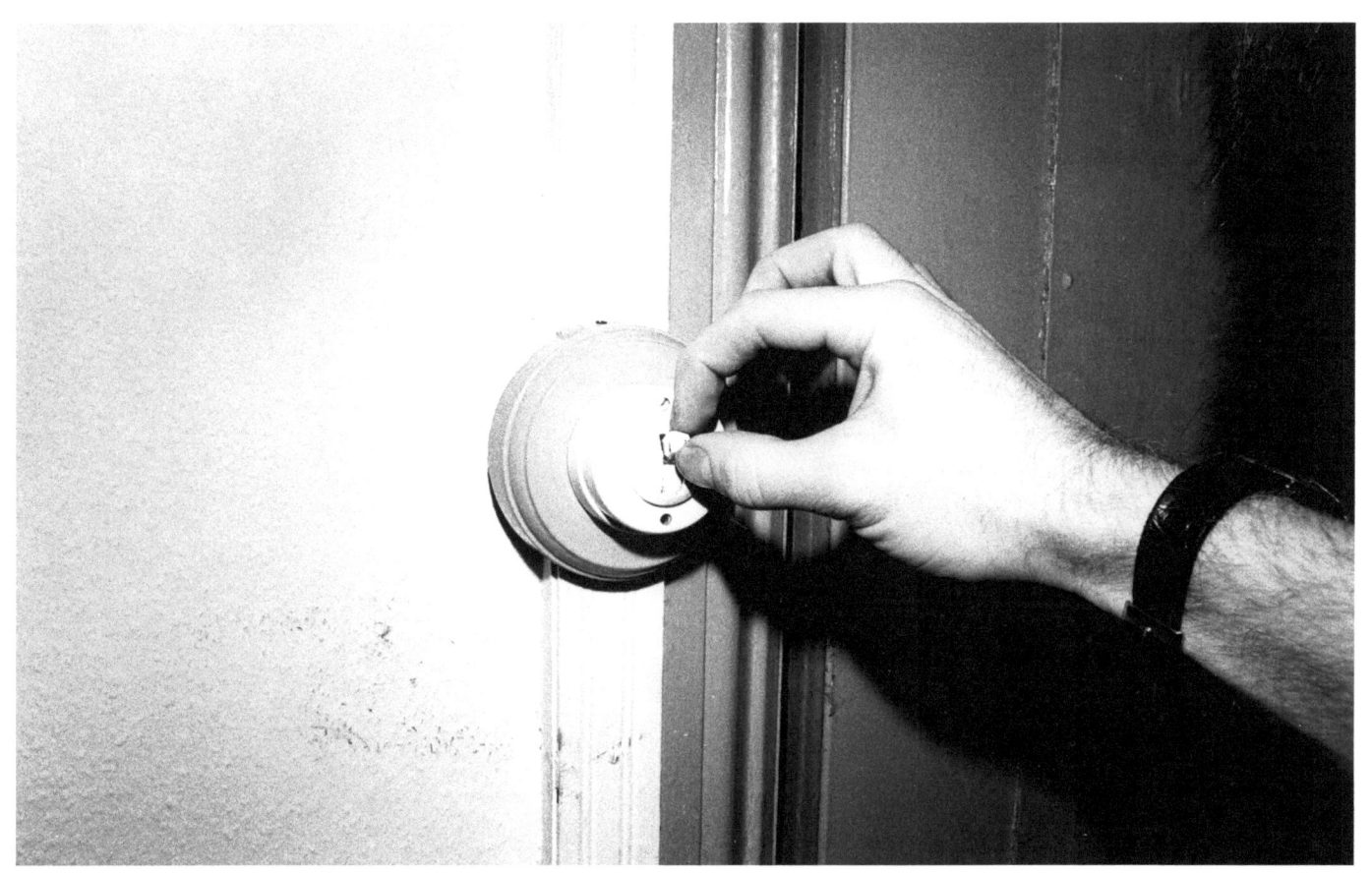

He prefers to light the bedroom.

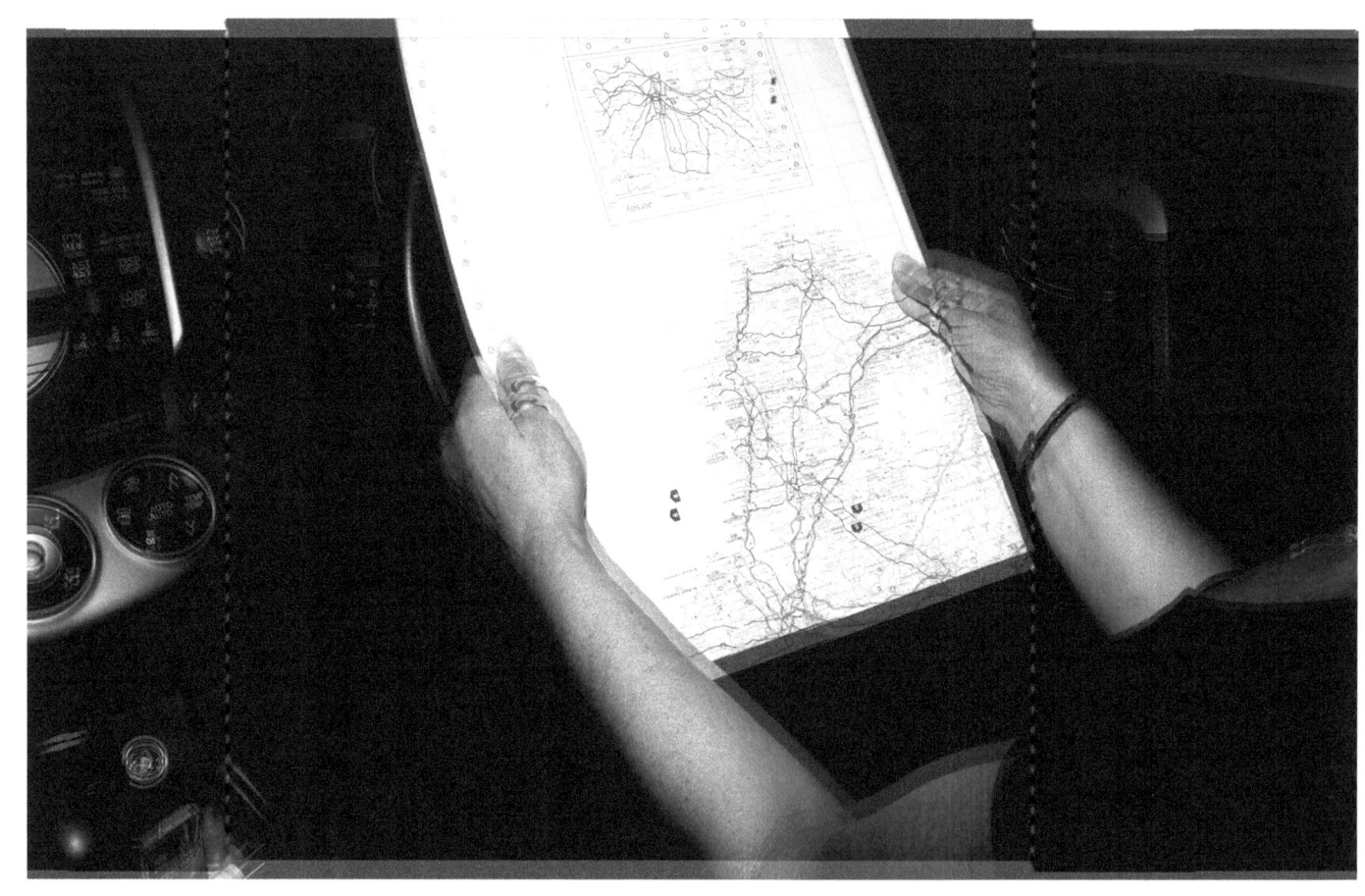

She occasionally had difficulty reading.
She occasionally had difficulty reading.

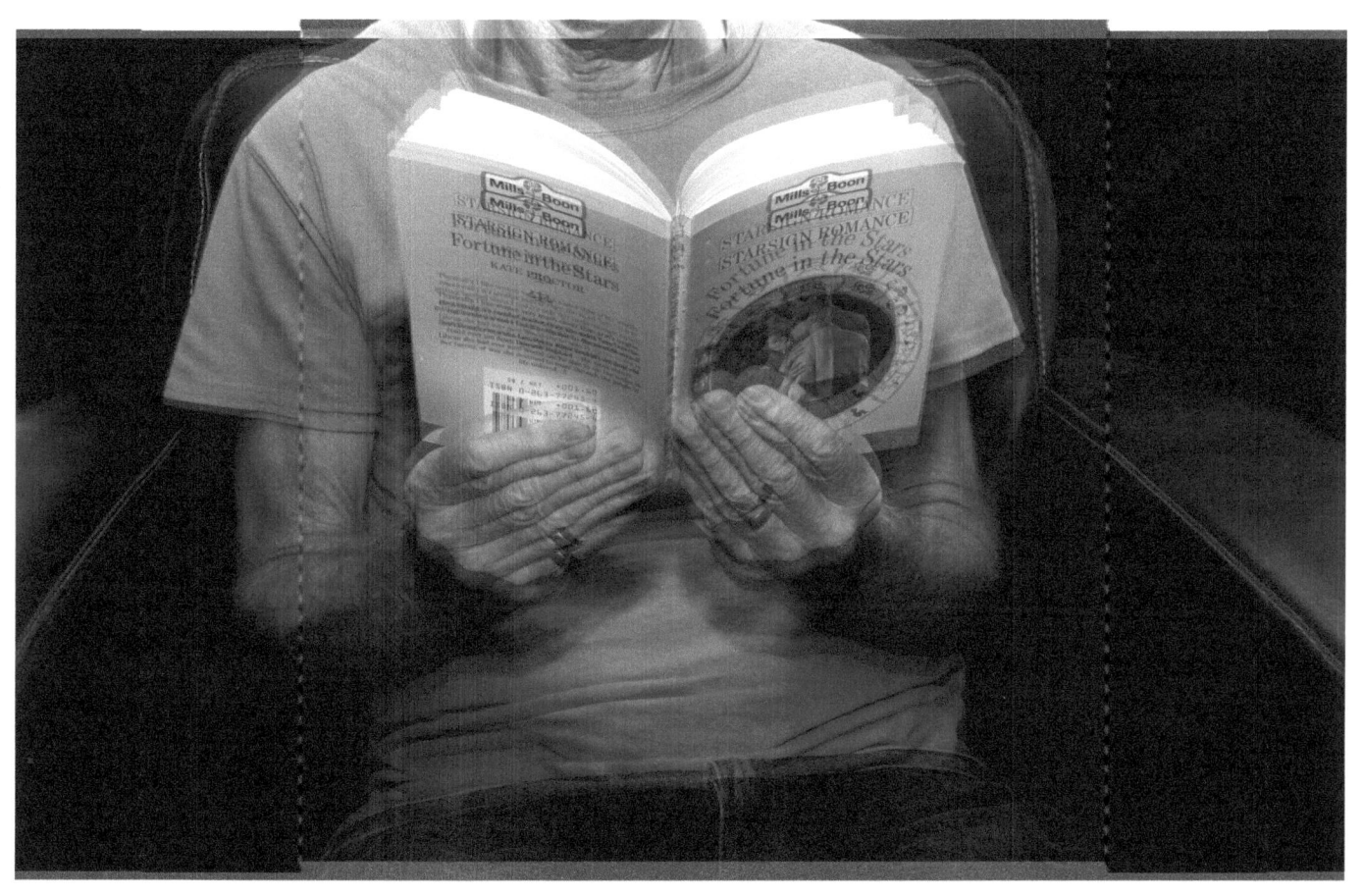

He occasionally had difficulty reading.

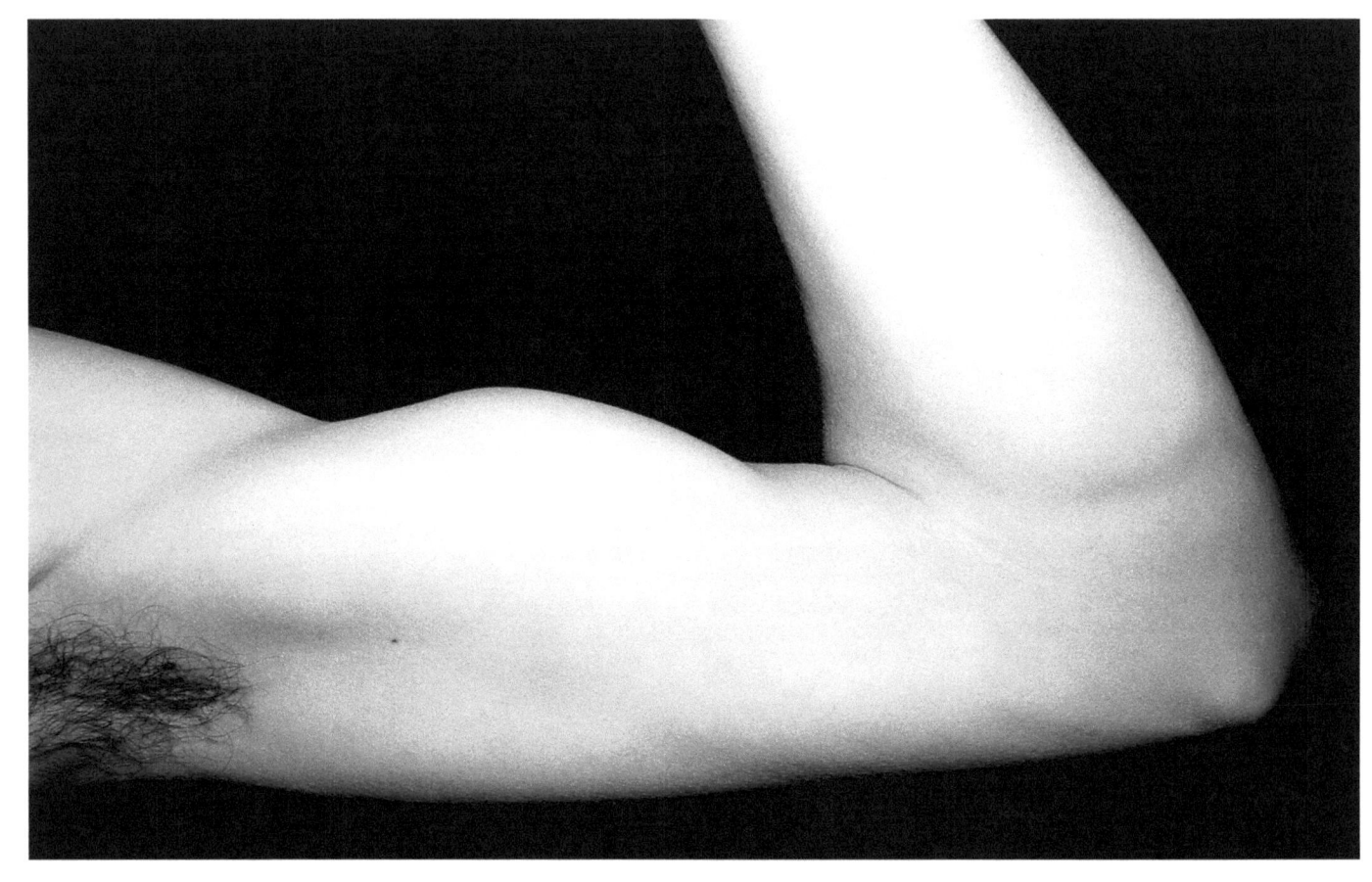

She desires curves.

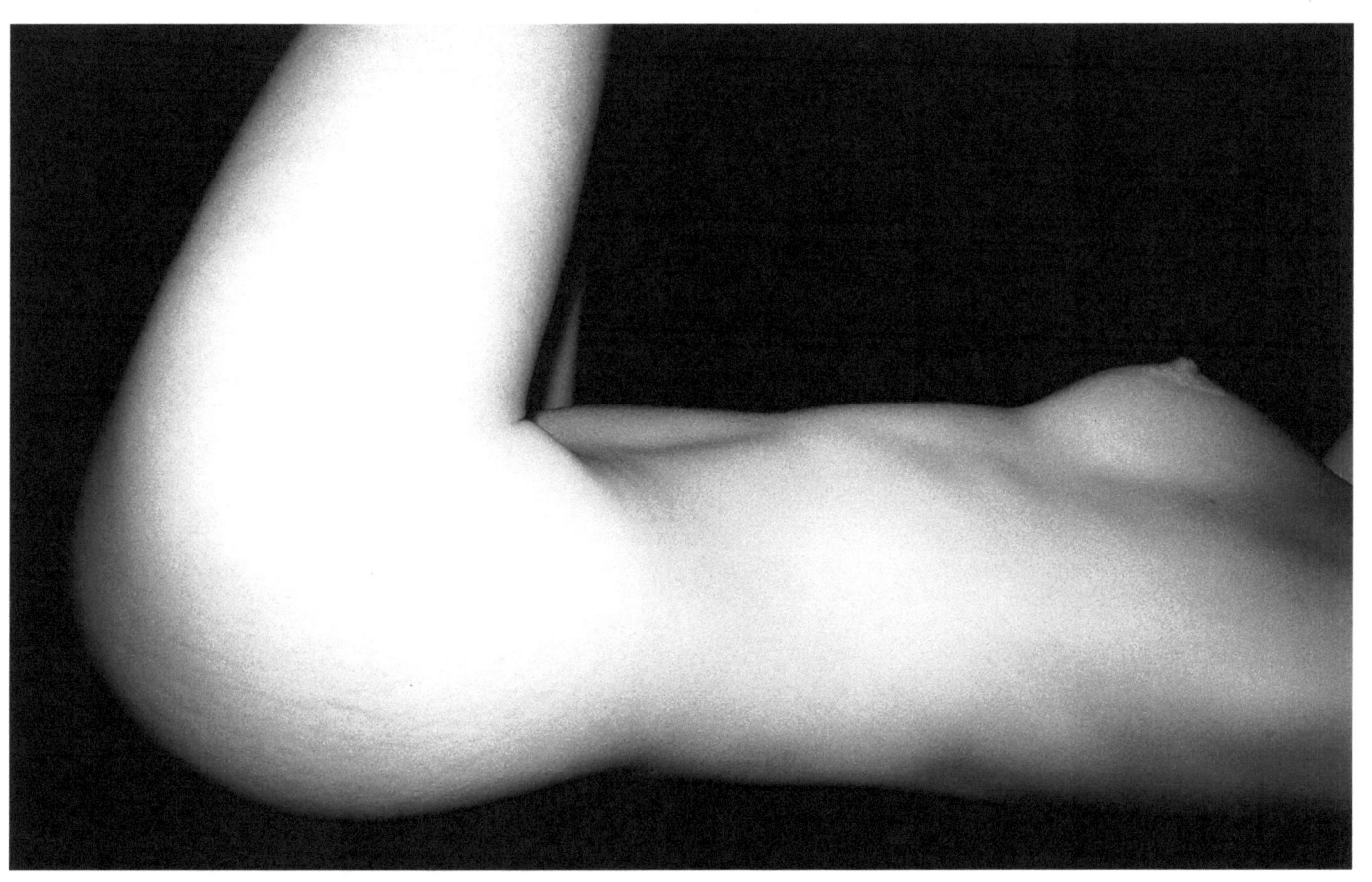

He desires curves.

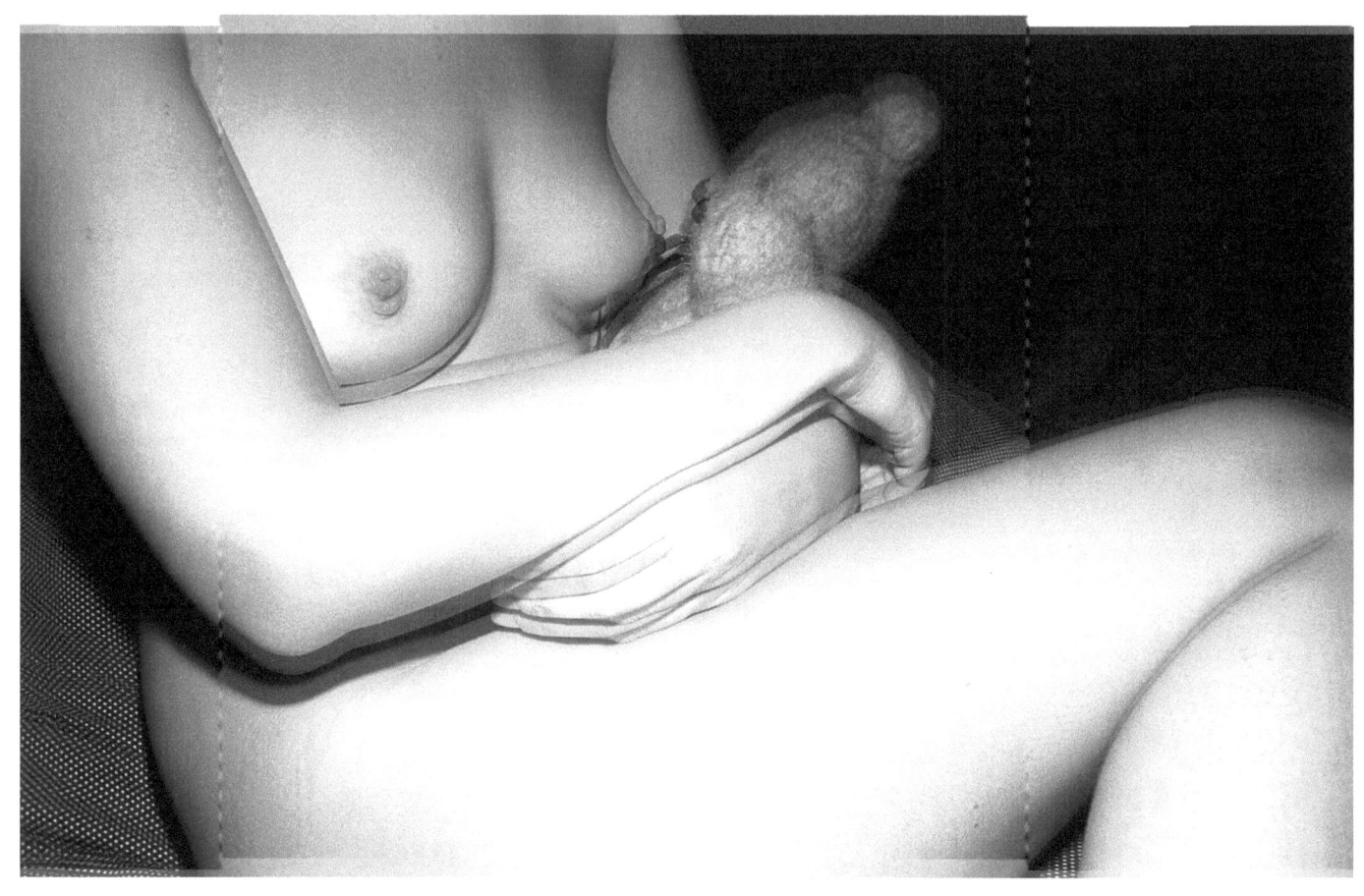

She is anxious about becoming a mother.
She is anxious about becoming a mother.

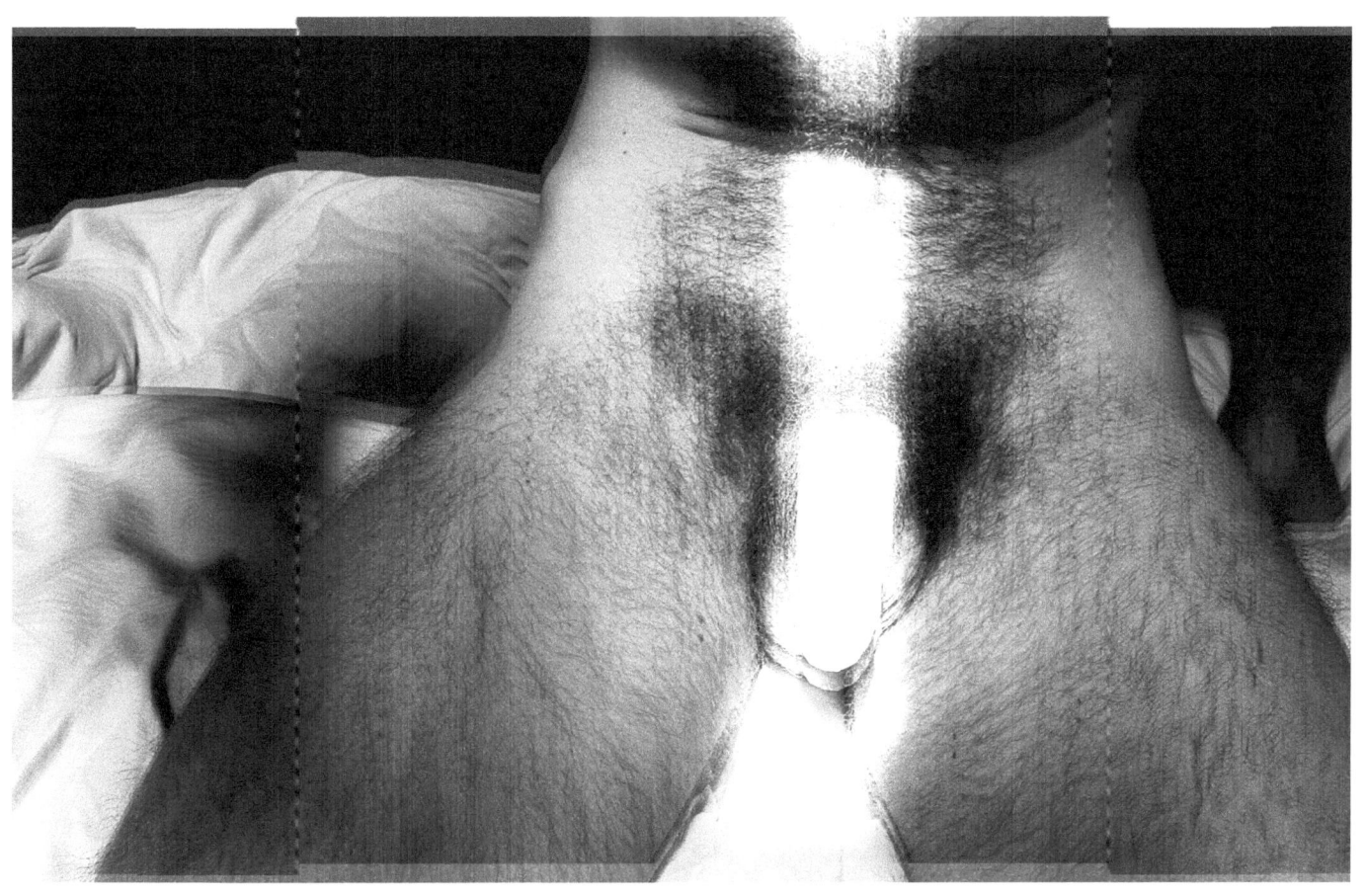

He is anxious about becoming a father.

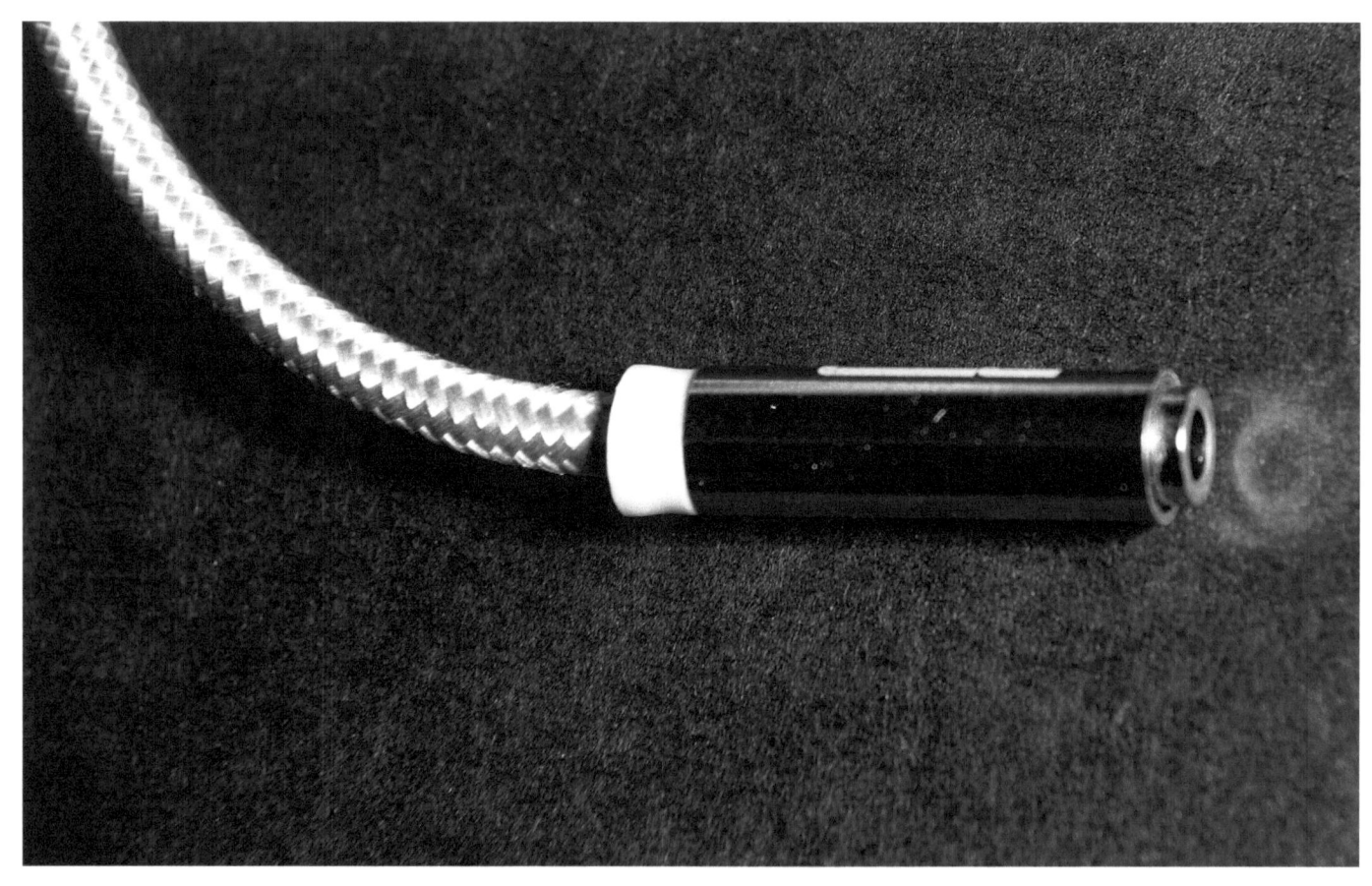

She identifies with this one.

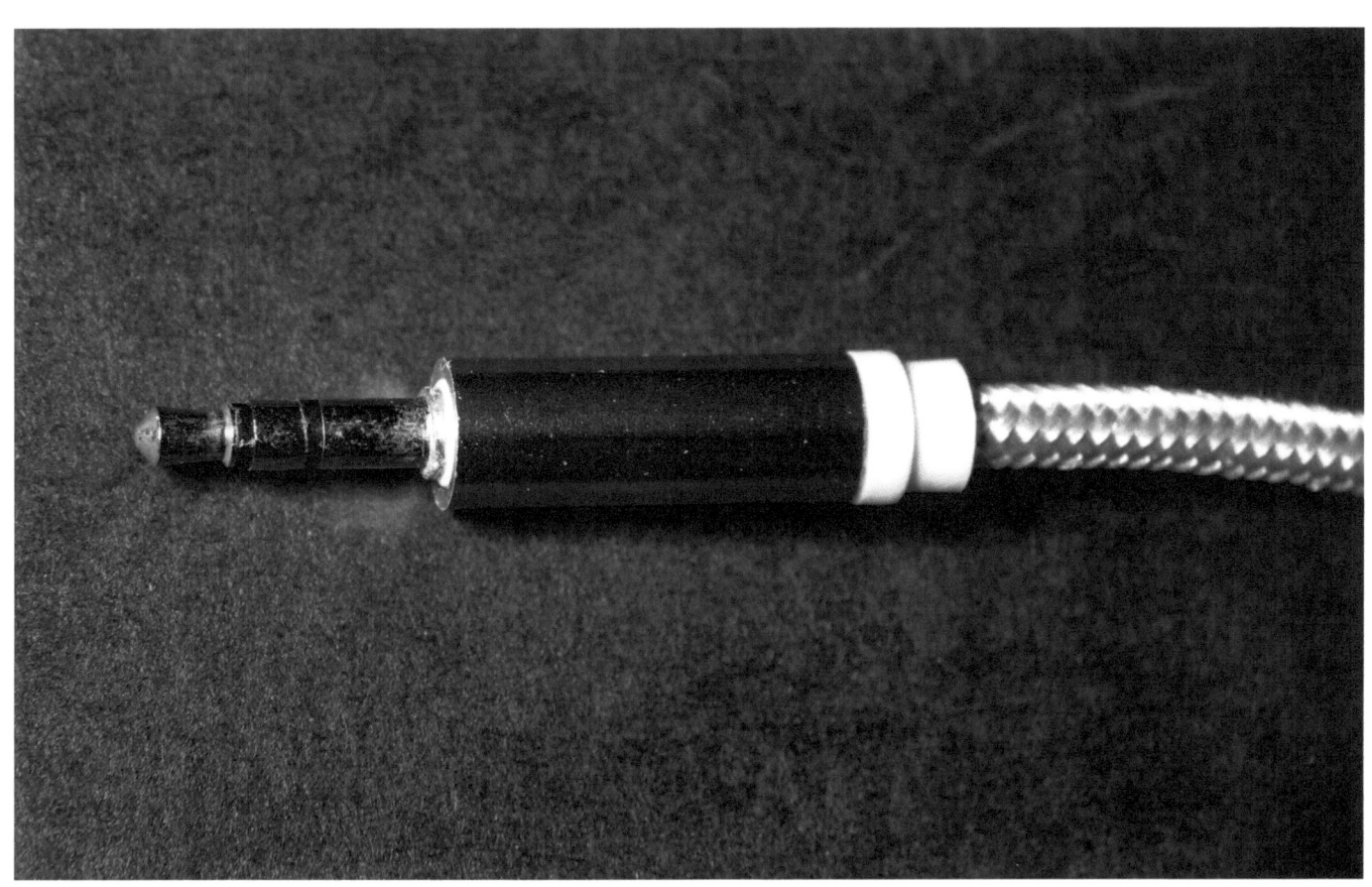

He identifies with this one.

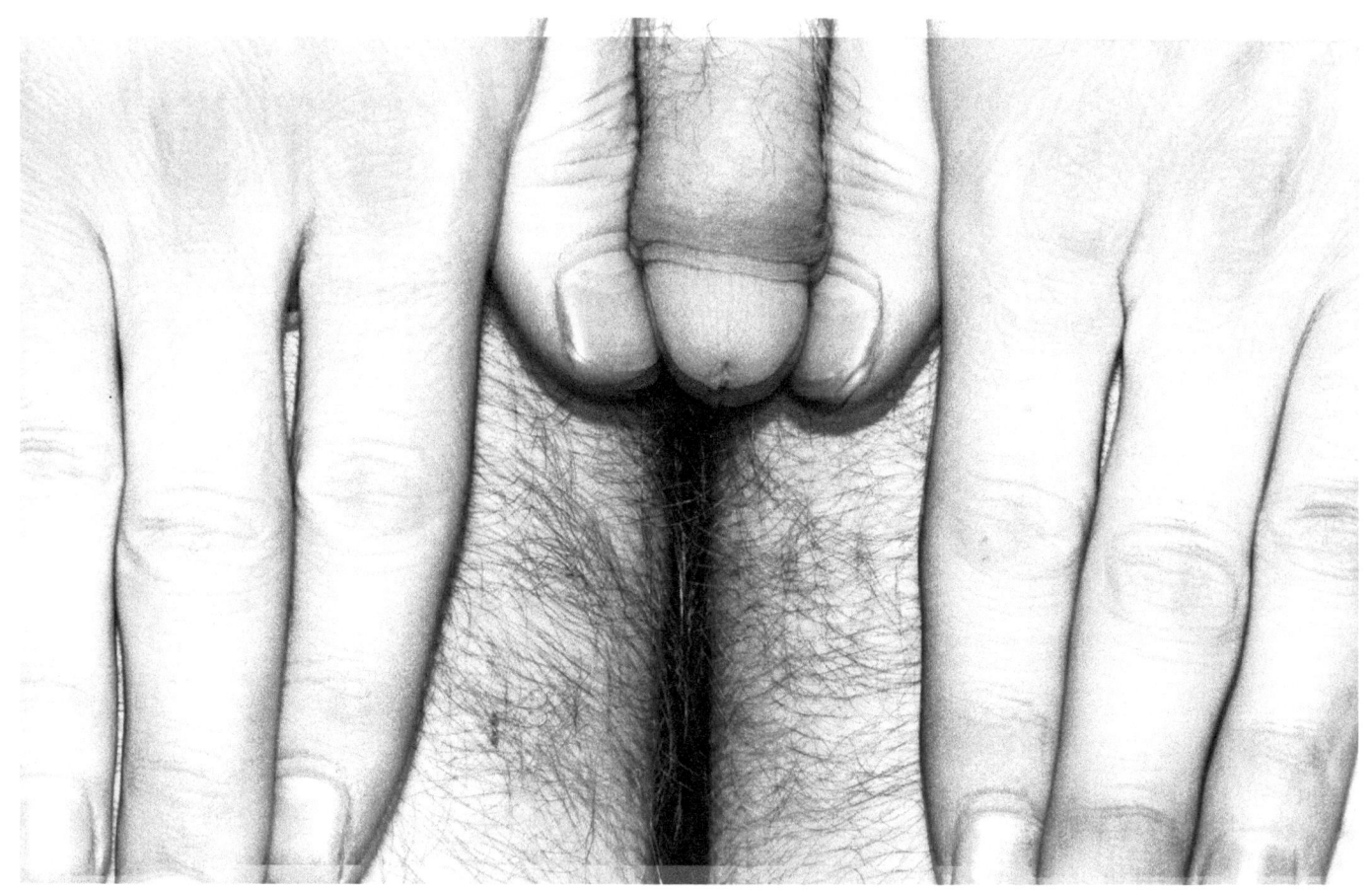

She thinks plus.
She thinks plus.

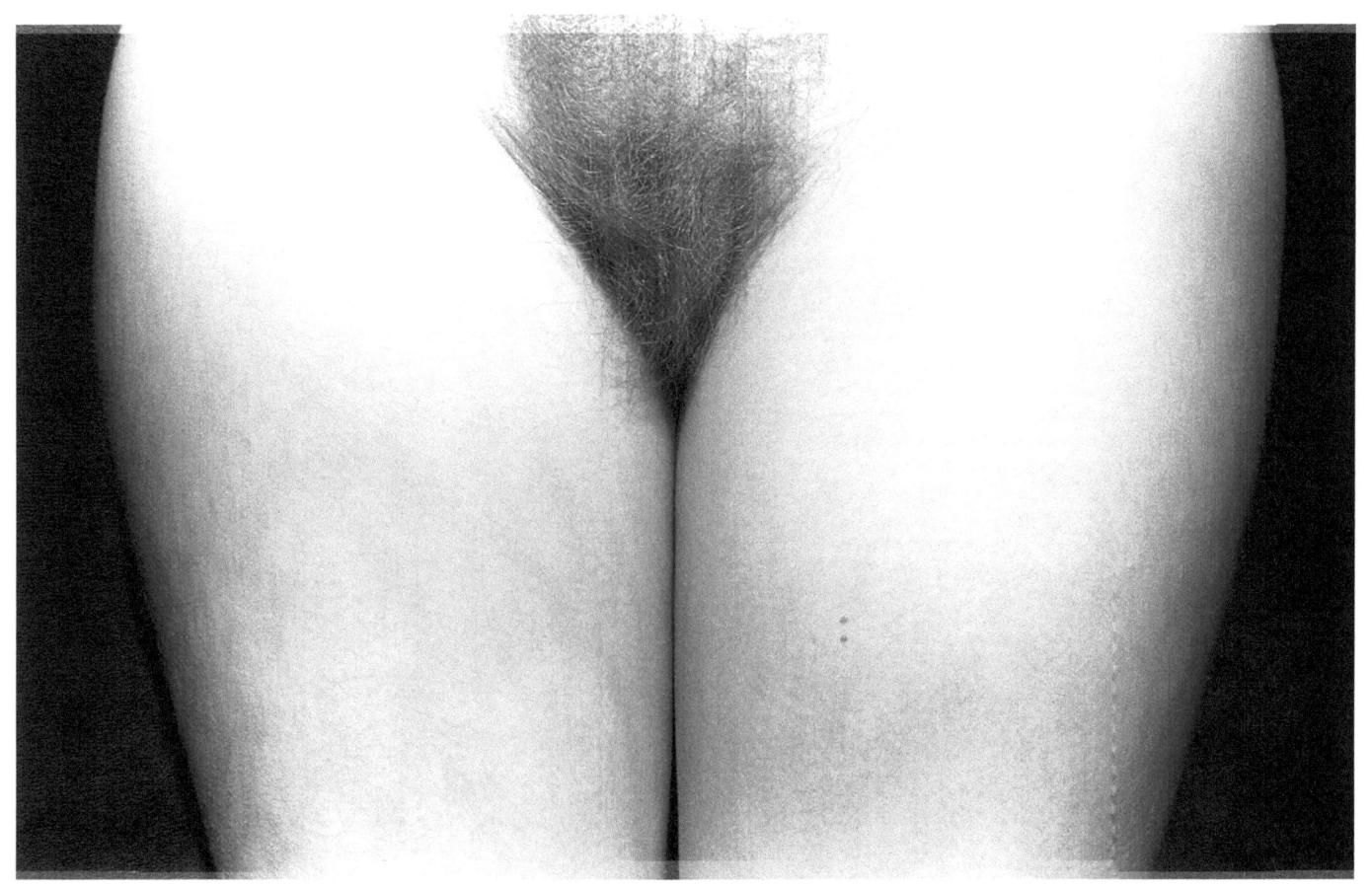

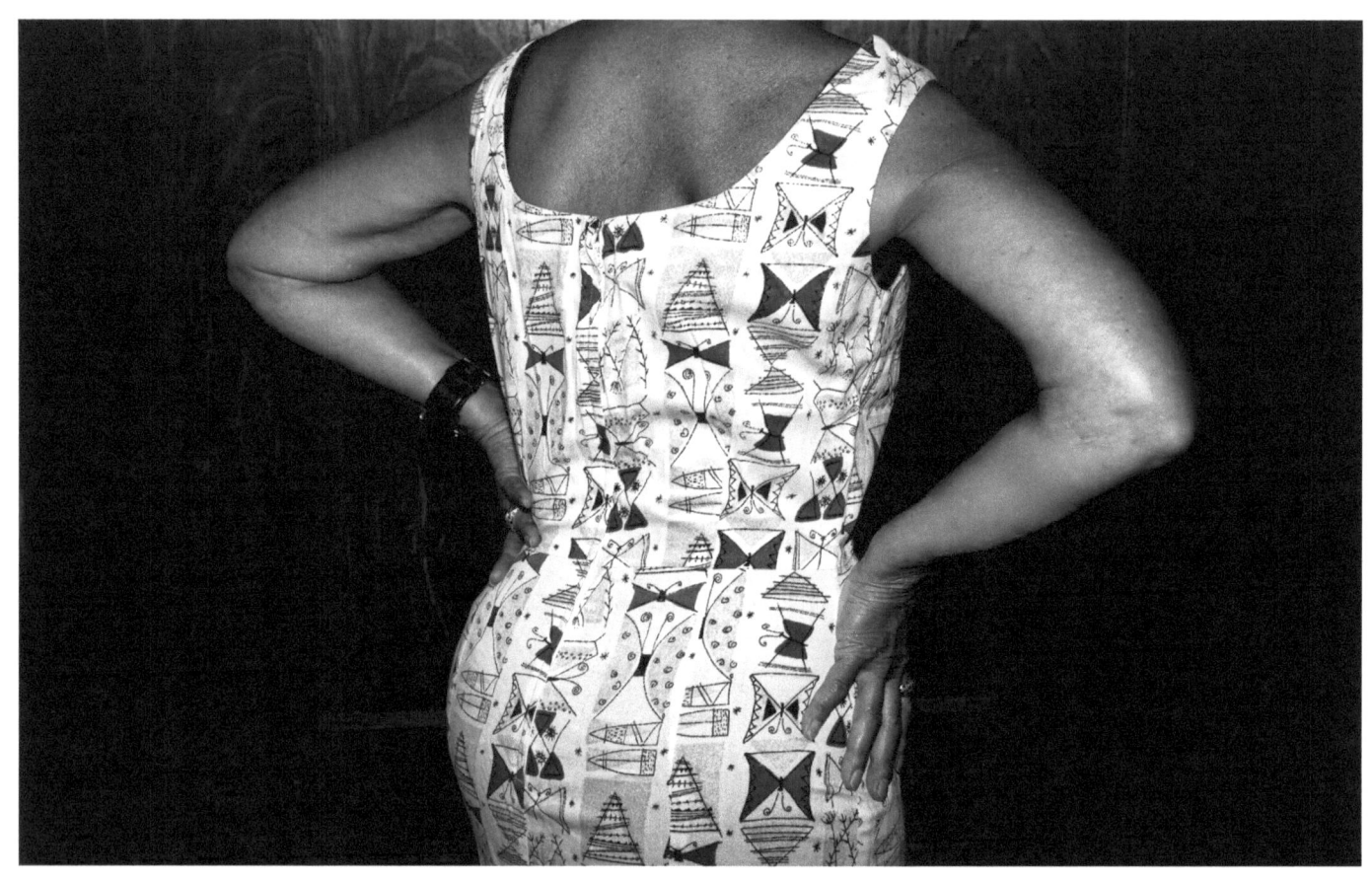

She wondered if her bum looked big in this.

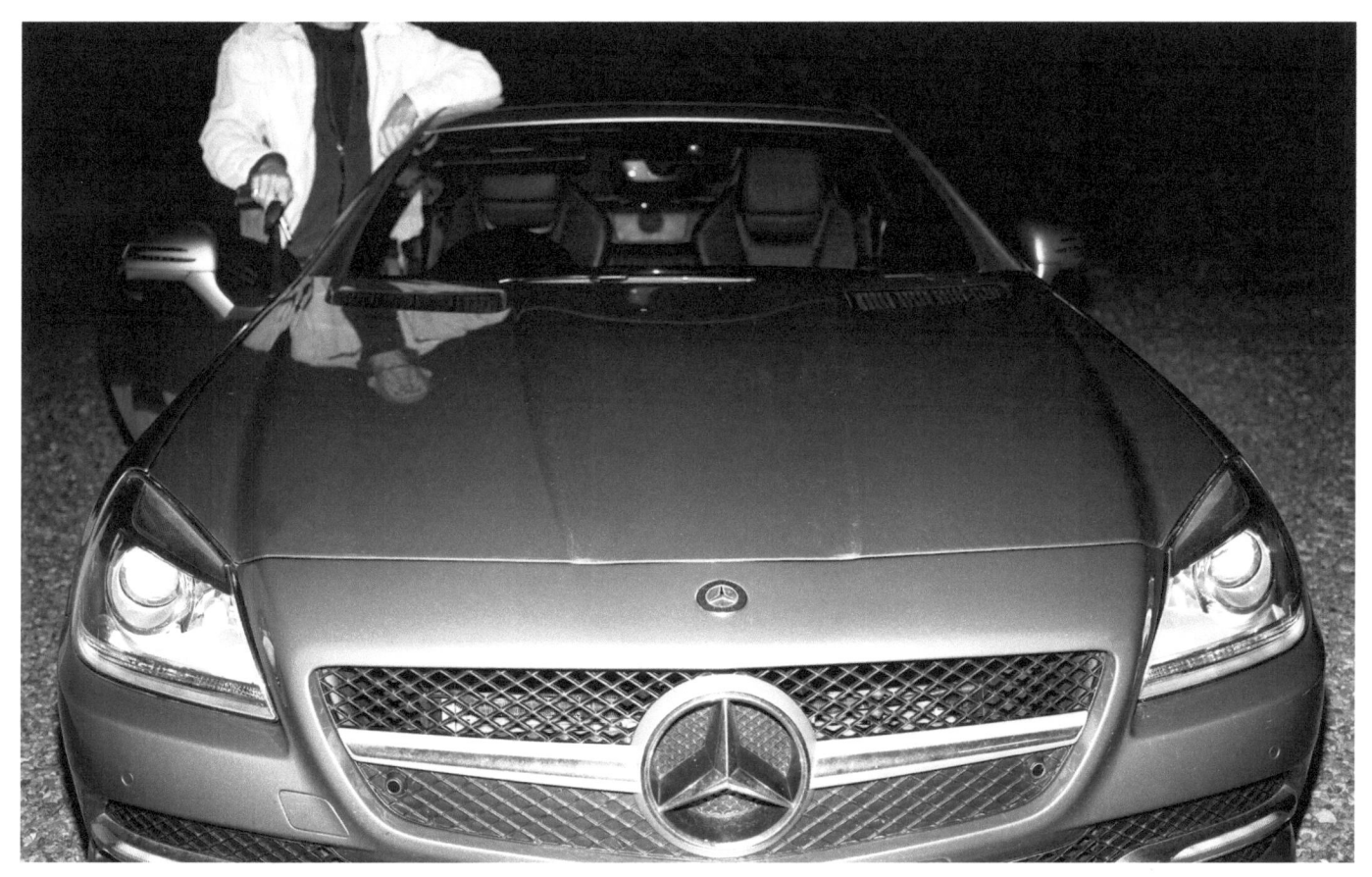

He wondered if his cock looked big in this.

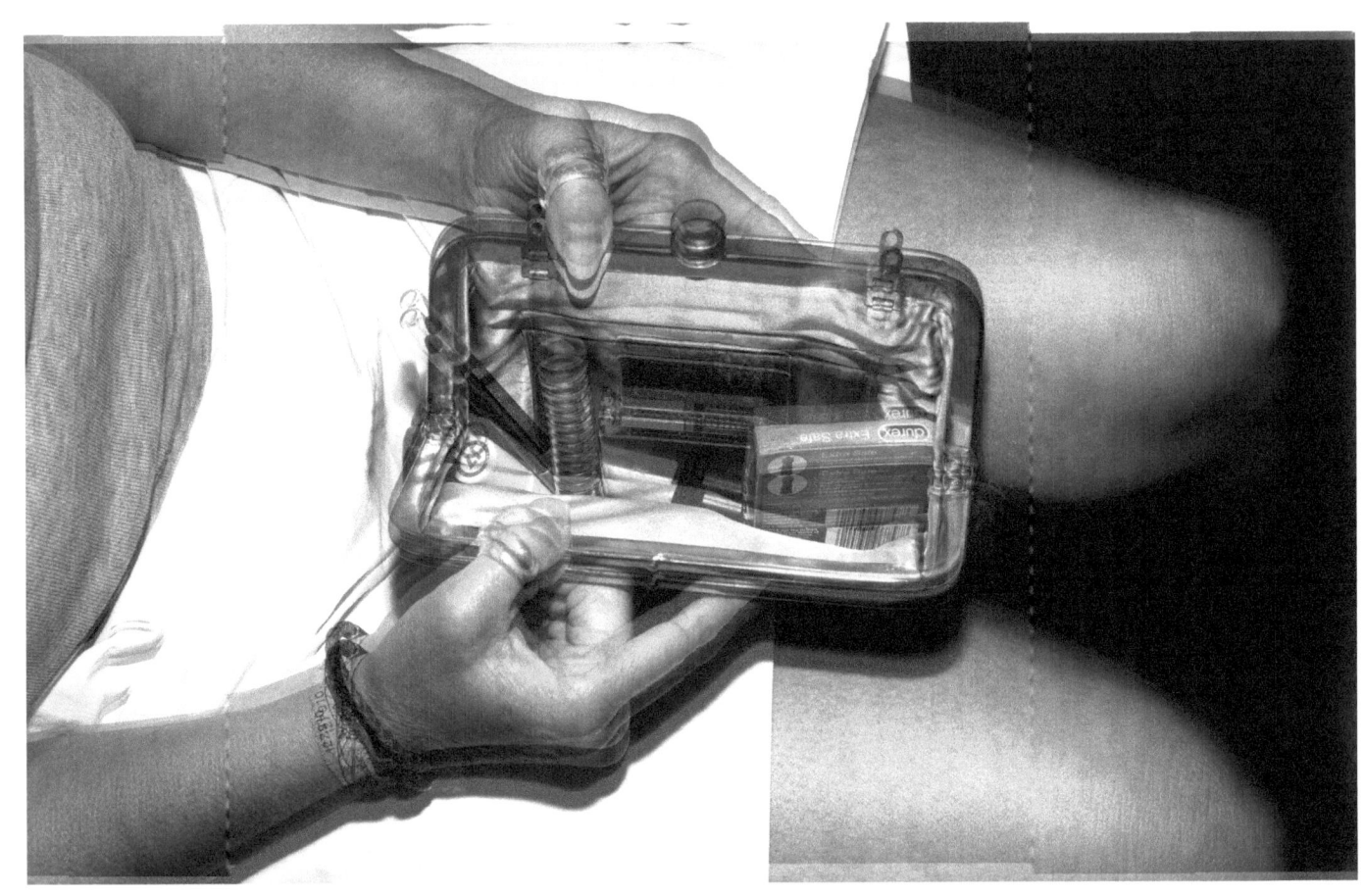

She has an idea what he wants from a relationship.
She has an idea what he wants from a relationship.

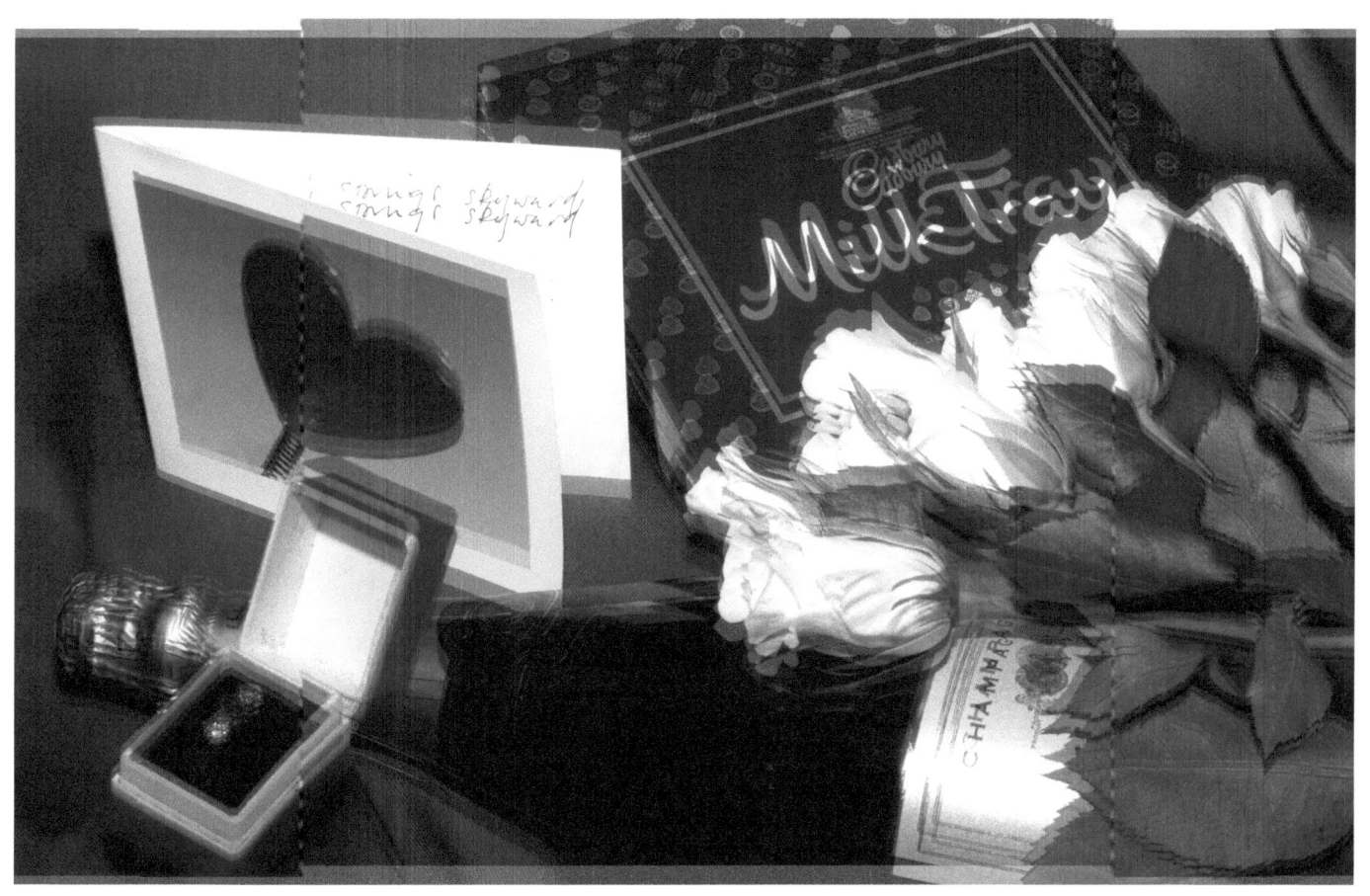

He has an idea what she wants from a relationship.

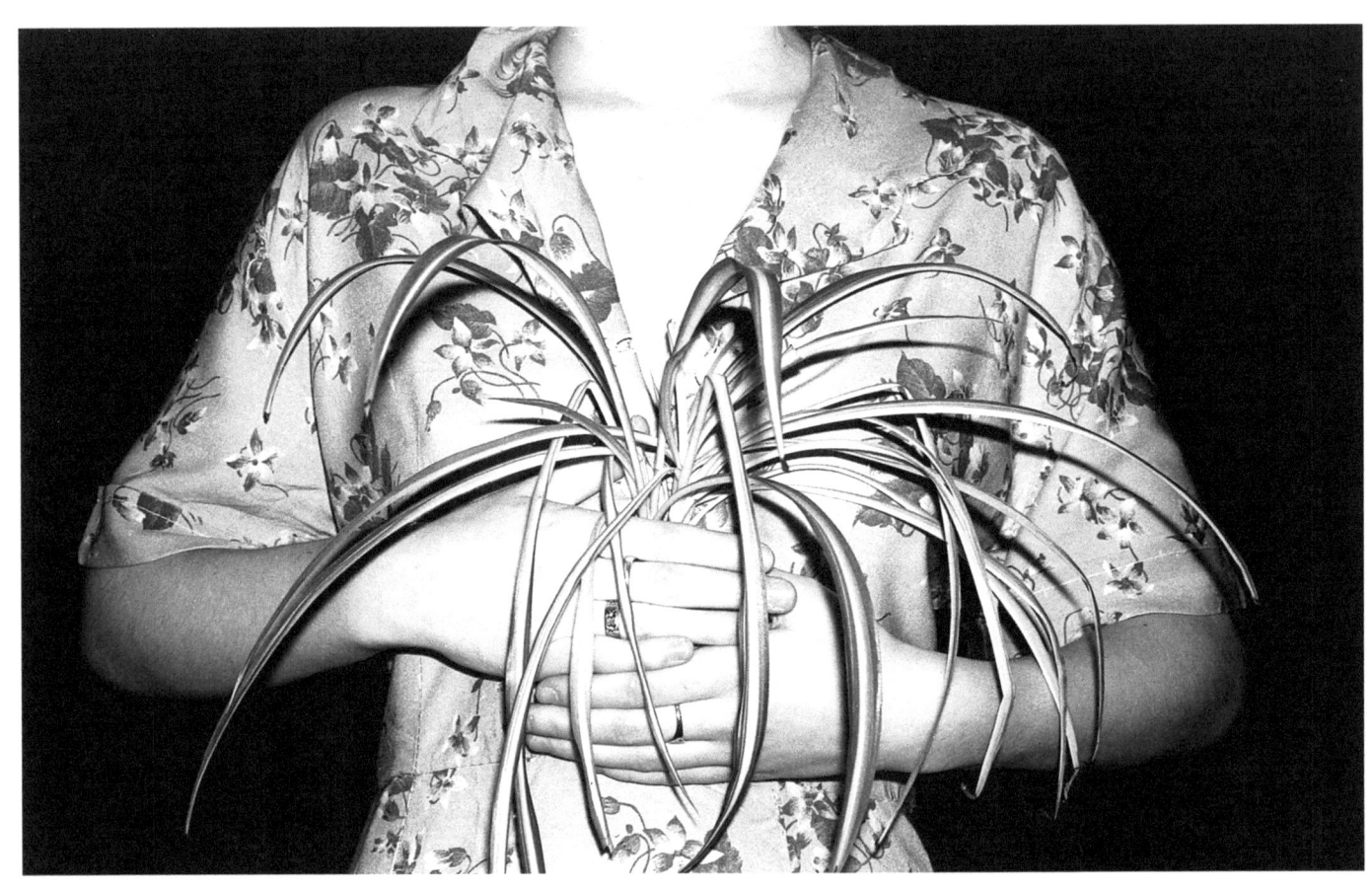

She sees beauty in natural forms.

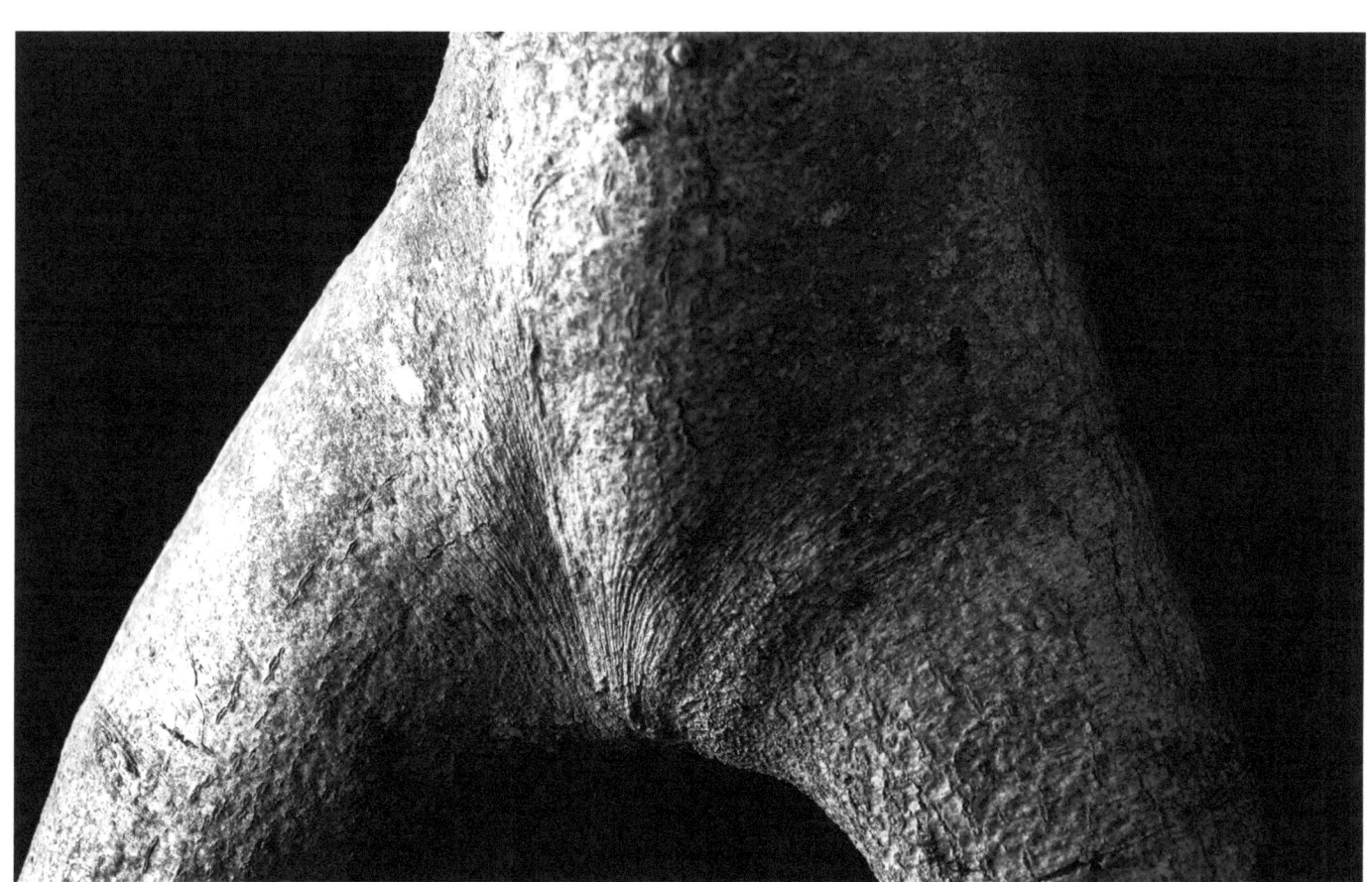

He sees beauty in natural forms.

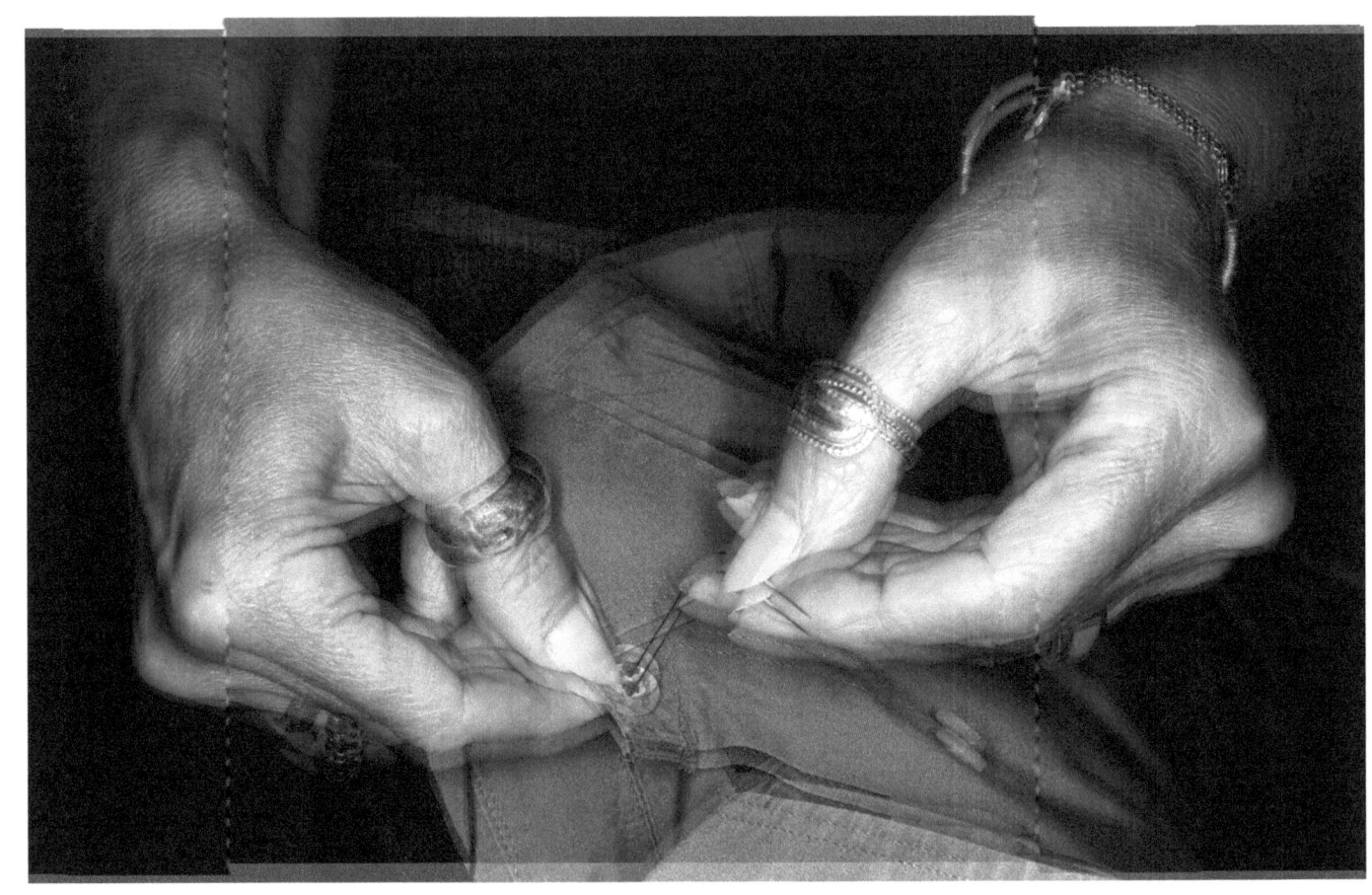

She dealt with any buttons.
She dealt with any buttons.

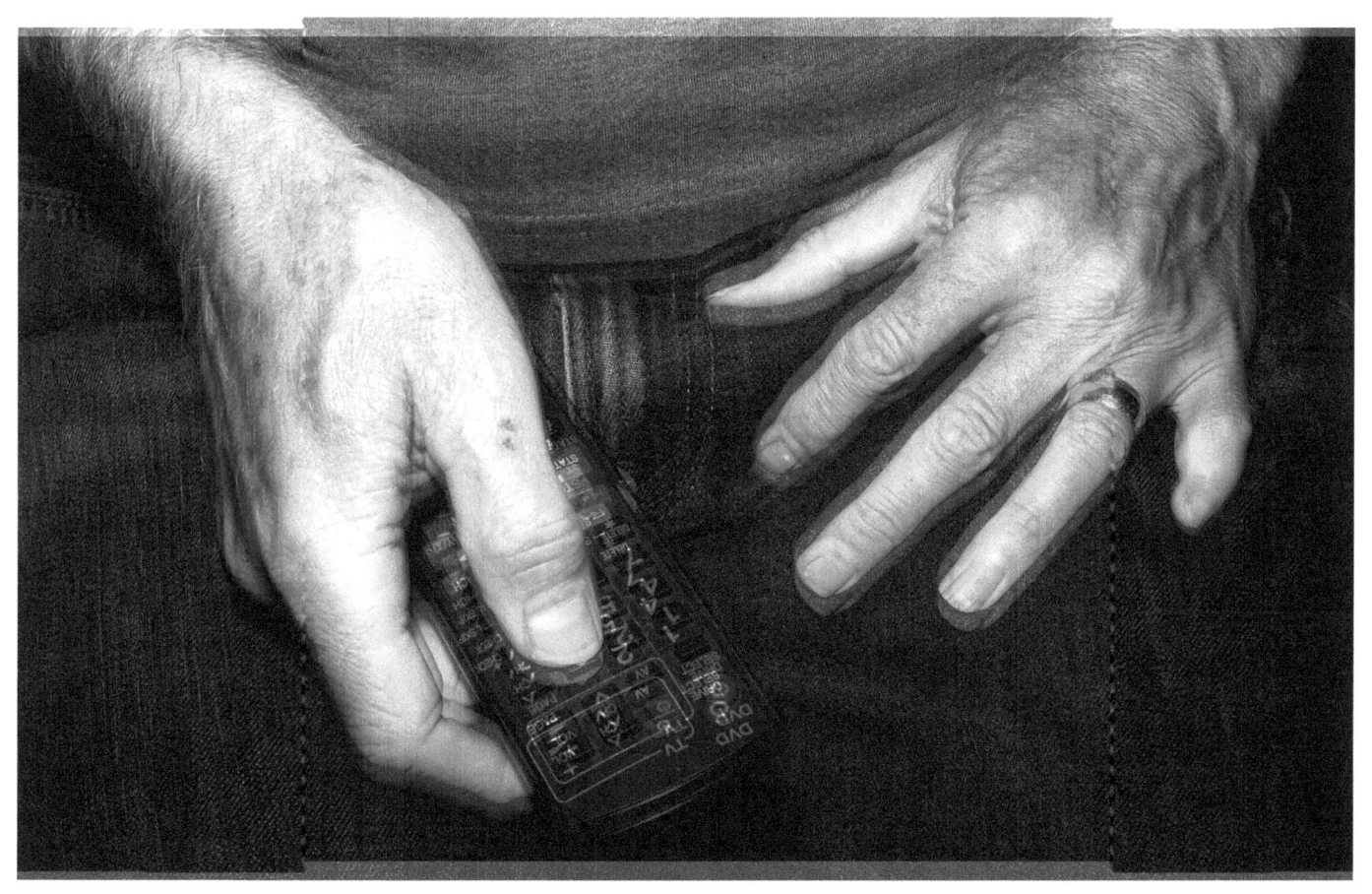

He dealt with any buttons.
He dealt with any buttons.

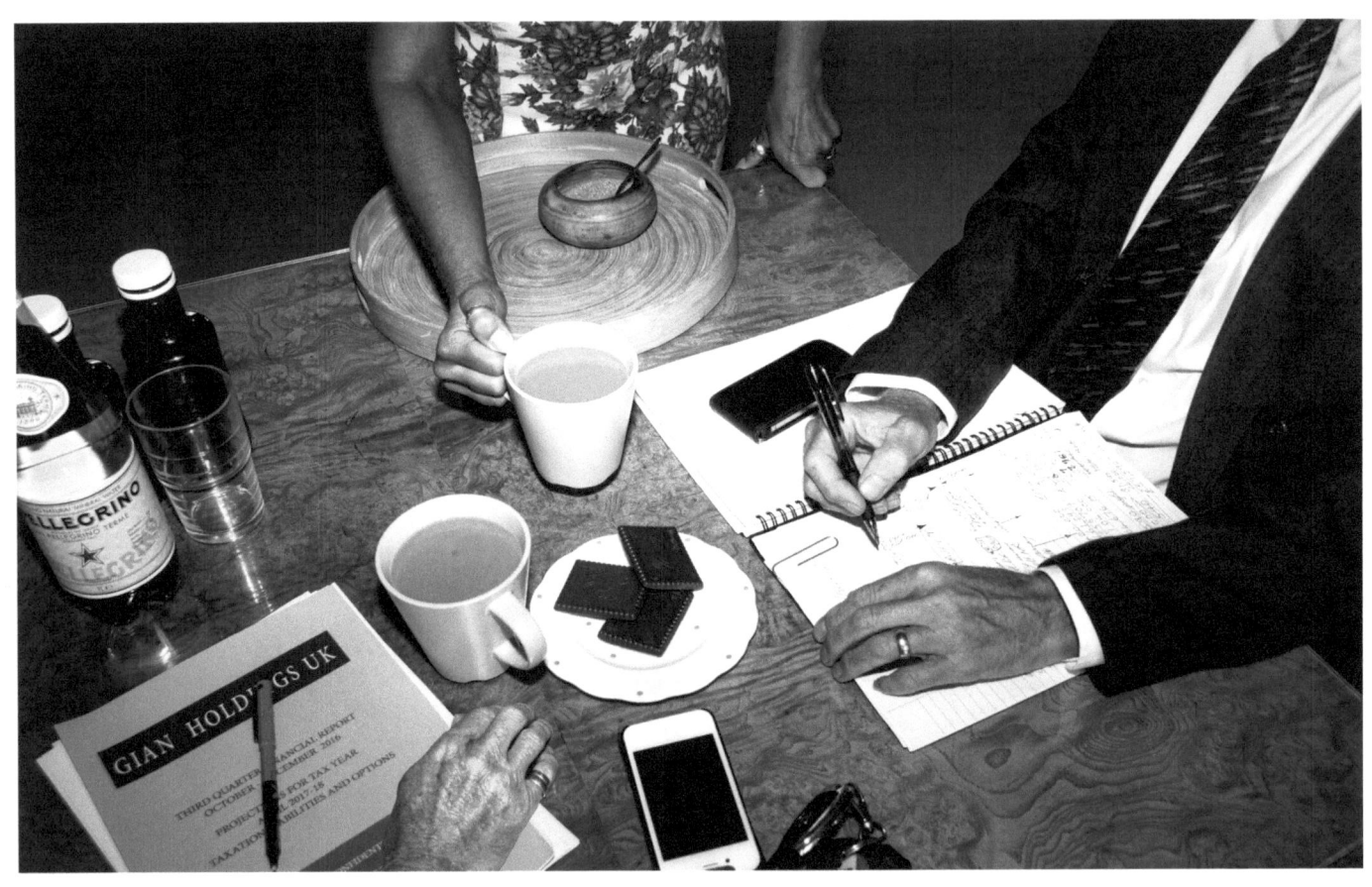

She serves her employer well.

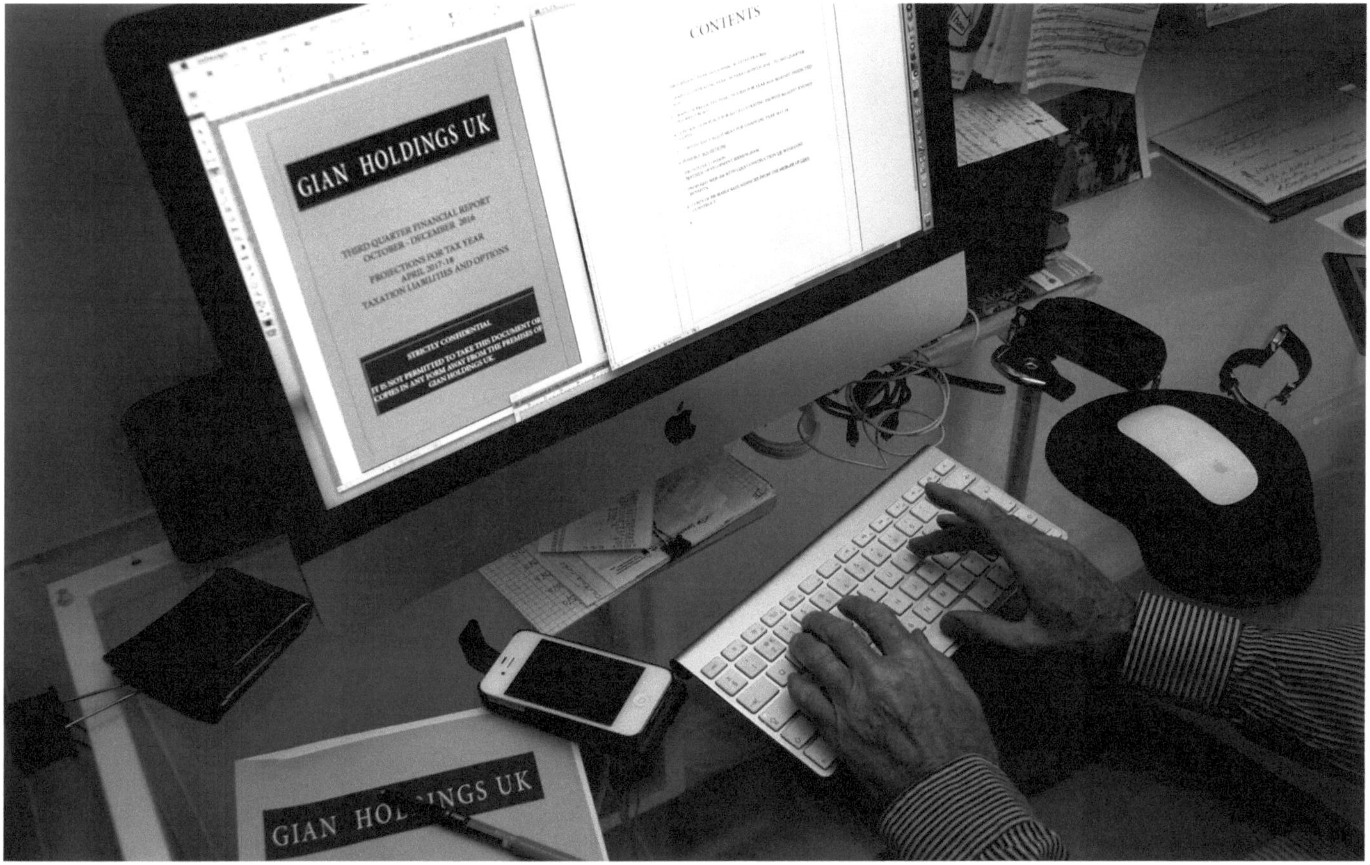

He serves his employer well.

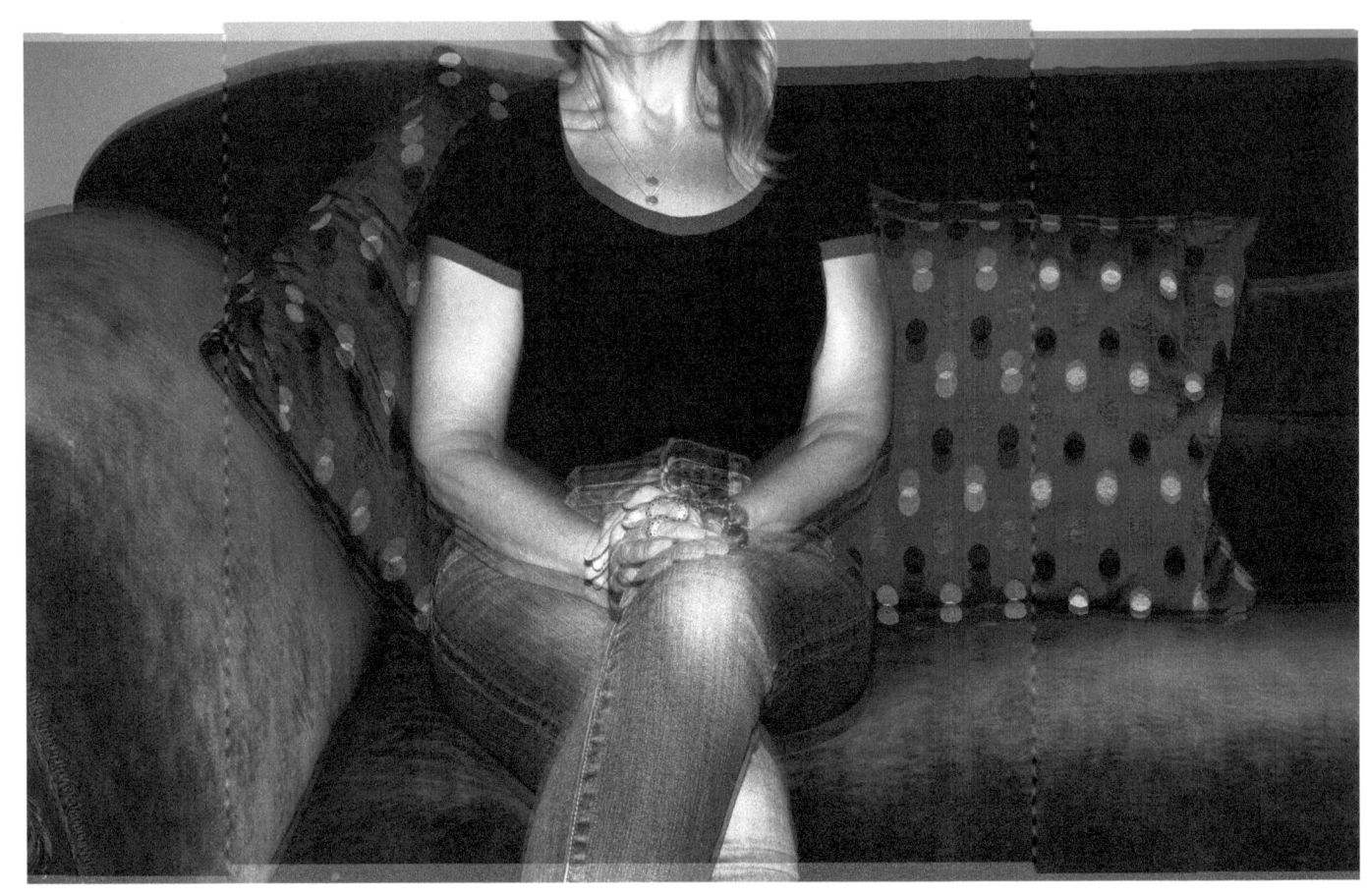

She relaxed when sitting down.
She relaxed when sitting down.

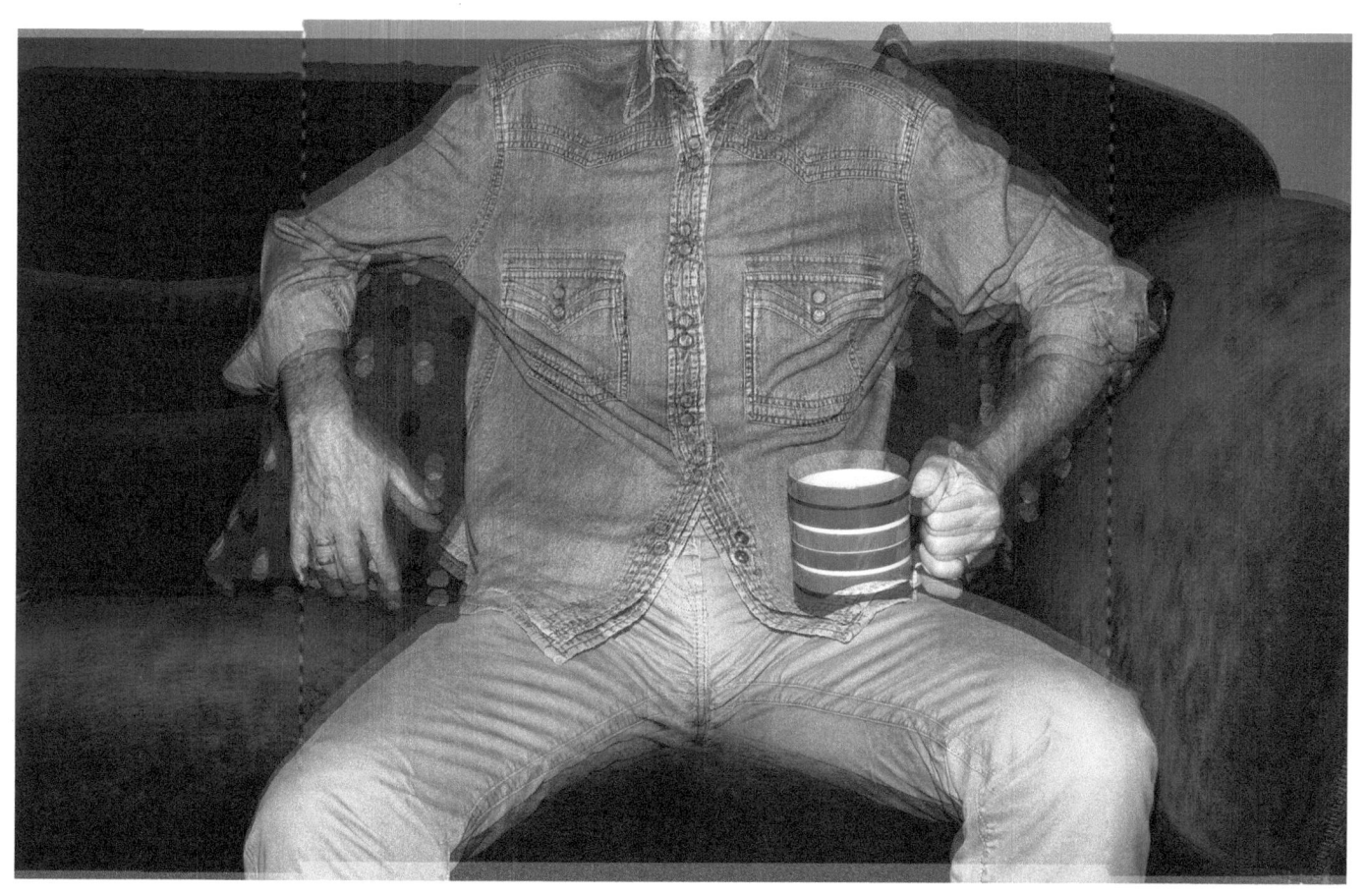

He relaxed when sitting down.
He relaxed when sitting down.

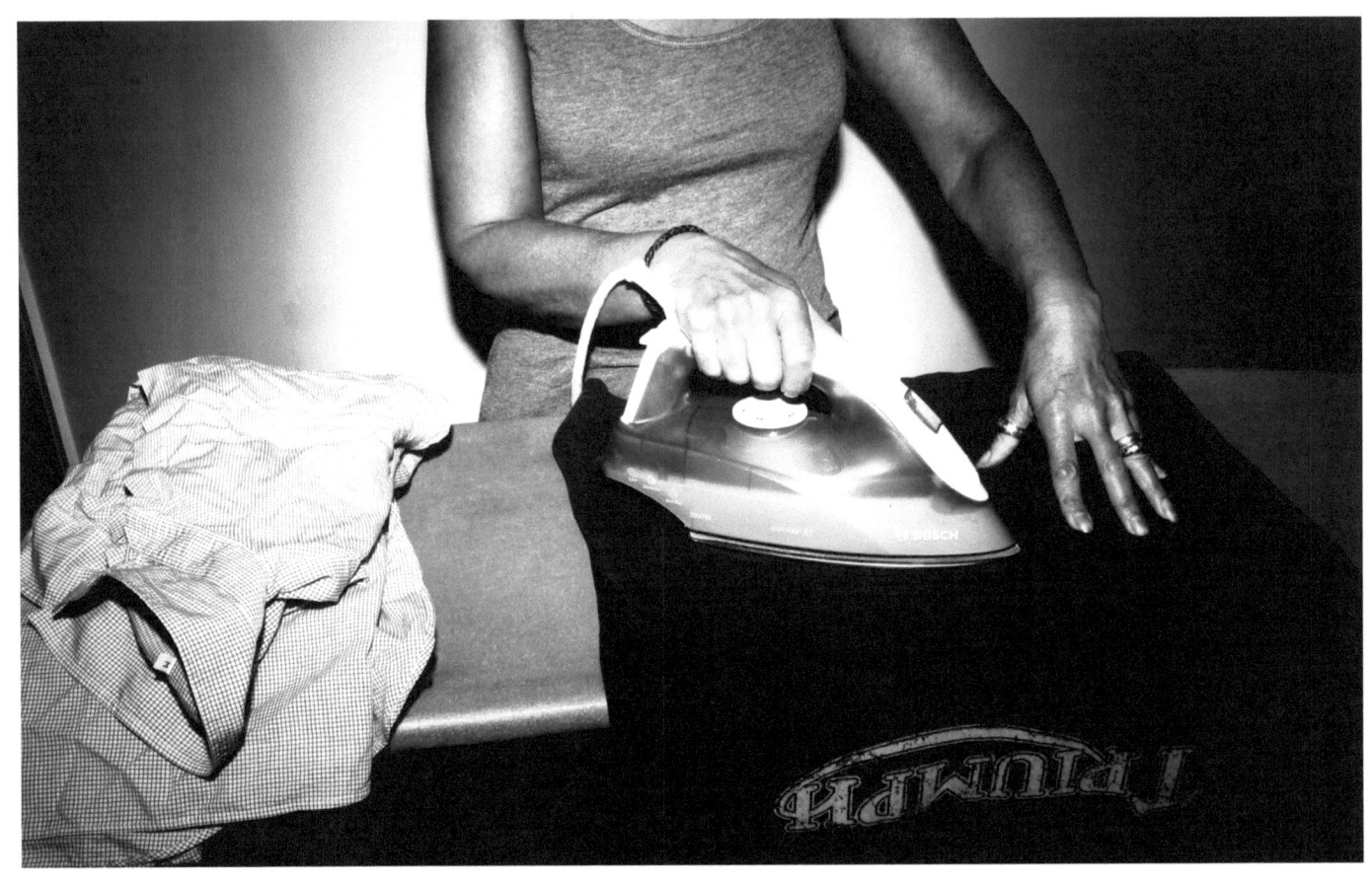

She knows a woman's work is never done.

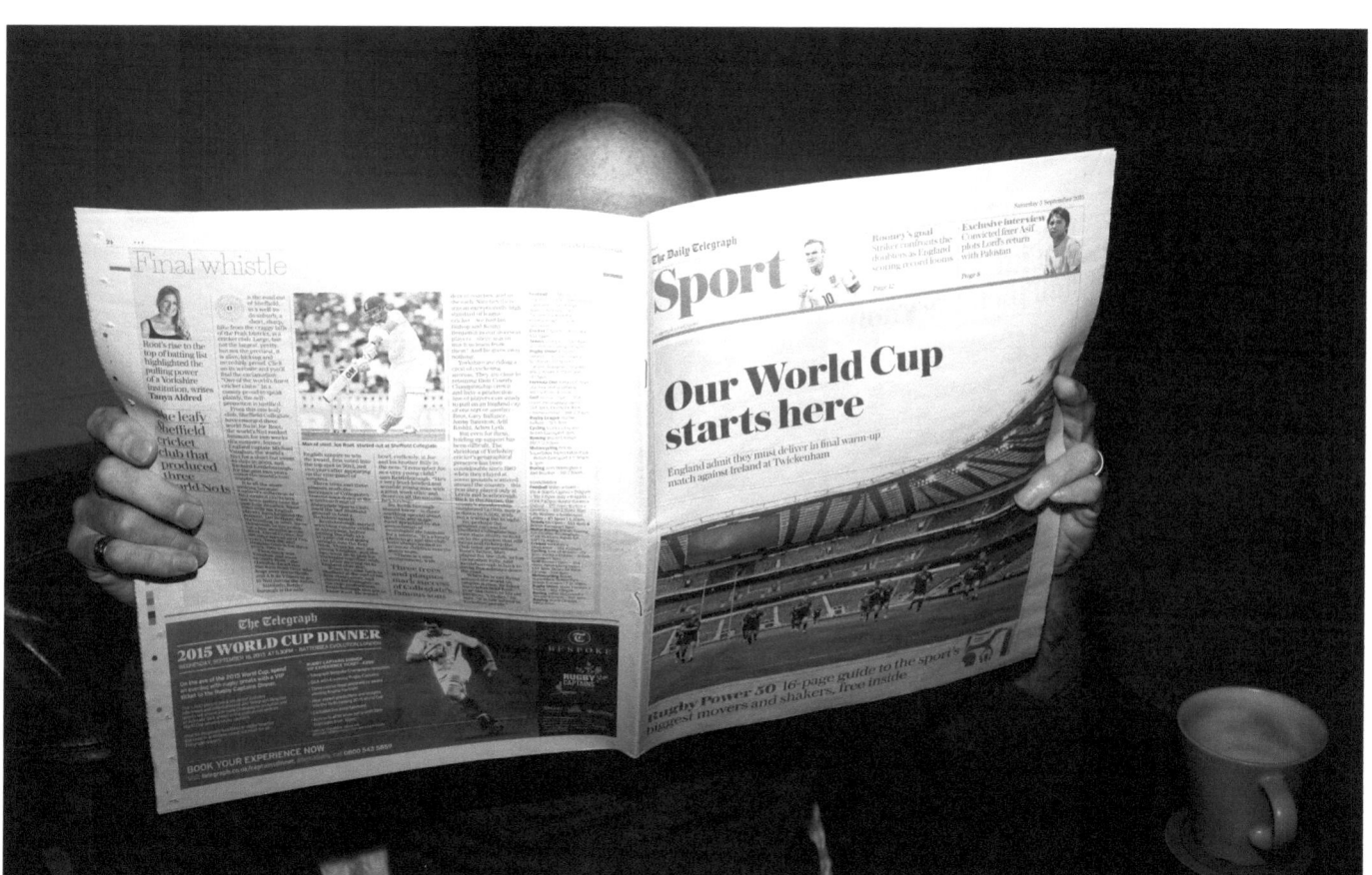

He knows a woman's work is never done.

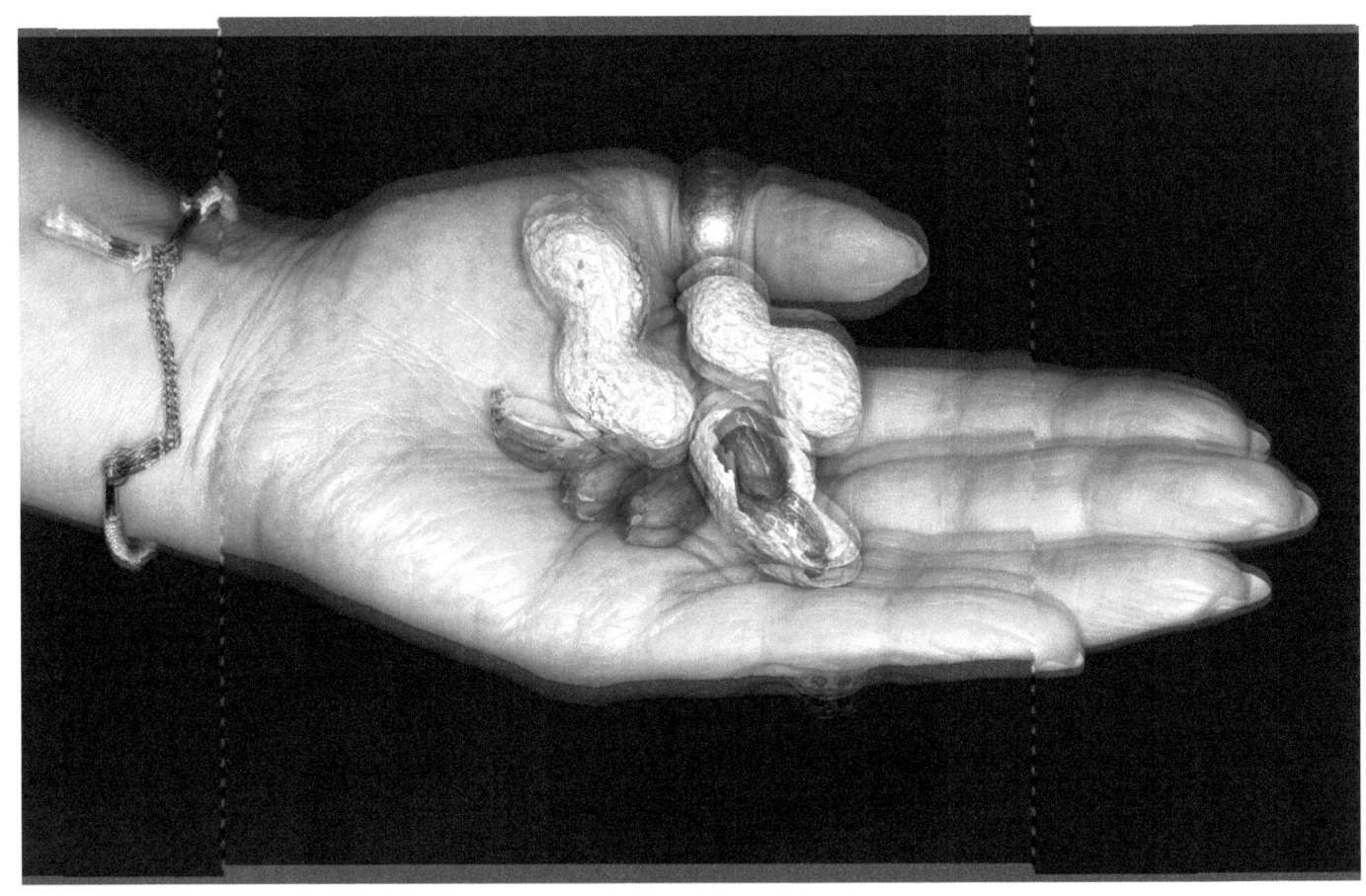

She earns money.
She earns money.

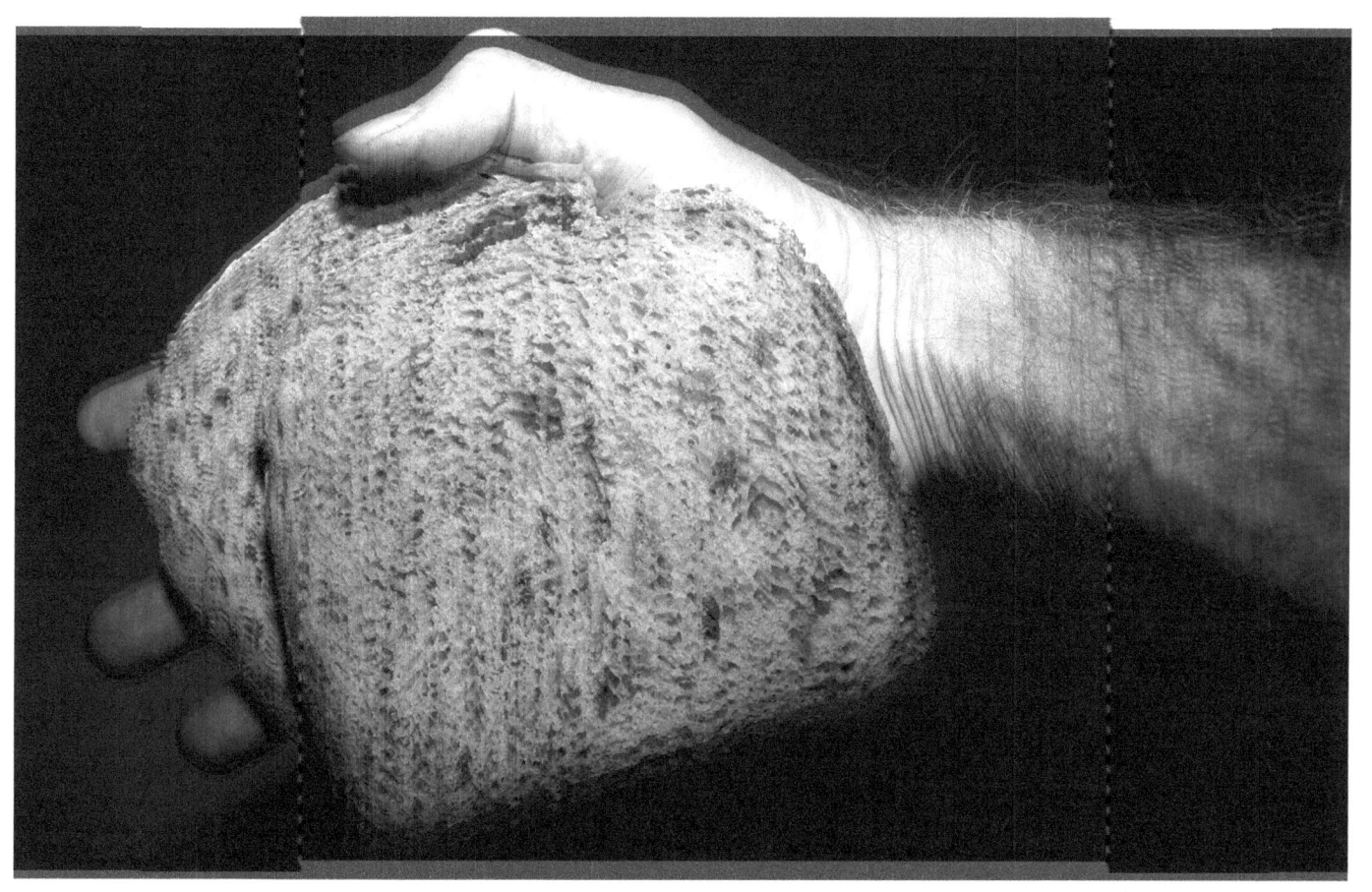

He earns money.
He earns money.